THE SHADE BOOK

How to Make Roller, Roman, Balloon, and Austrian Shades

by Judy Lindahl

.d names are mentioned in this book only to indicate
onsumer products which I have personally used and
with which I have been pleased. There may be other
products that are comparable or even better about which
I am unaware.

About the Author: Judy Lindahl is a free lance home econo-
mist residing in Portland, Oregon. She was graduated from
Washington State University with honors and received her
B.S. in Home Economics Education. After graduation she
taught home economics in Beaverton, Oregon for several
years before leaving to join the educational staff at Sim-
plicity Pattern Company, Inc. of New York. As an educational fashion stylist Judy traveled the country presenting
programs in schools and for 4-H, extension, and consumer
groups for five and a half years. In 1973 she created a pro-
gram of ideas and inspiration for do-it-yourself decorators
which she has presented across the country and in Canada.
She is the author and publisher of Decorating with Fabric/
An Idea Book (paperback) which grew out of the programs,
and Decorating with Fabric, a hardback for Butterick Pub-
lishing. Judy has also done writing, television, and dem-
onstration work for Fieldcrest sheets. Currently Judy teaches
and travels on a free lance basis. She is married and the
mother of two daughters and has been featured in Outstand-
ing Young Women of America and Personalities of the West
and Midwest.

CONTENTS

INTRODUCTION

You are about to discover the excitement, and the economy of making your own shades! There are so many to choose from, so many uses it almost boggles the mind. But the joy and accomplishment of creating for your own decor soon smooths away any hesitation.

Roller and Roman shades have a lot in common--they require approximately the same amount of fabric, they create essentially window-size treatments, they must be square in order to hang straight, they both have a flat appearance when lowered. But while most of the roller shade disappears when it is raised, more of the Roman will remain showing because of the space required for pleats to stack up.

For window treatments each of the shade types may be used alone or combined with a valance or cornice, cafe or draw curtains, side panels or shutters. Such versatility makes decorating a pleasure.

One of the best reasons to decorate with shades is that they can efficiently help to save energy. More detailed information is contained in the next chapter.

Shades can also give protection. Installed on south or west facing windows, shades help cut down exposure to sunlight which can be damaging to fabrics and wood finishes.

In addition to their uses at windows shades can replace cupboard or closet doors, hide shelves and storage, conceal laundry equipment or a sewing center, serve as room dividers and fill other functional answers to decorating obstacles. They can be adapted to most any area in a short amount of time.

1

If all of these reasons are not enough to convince you that you'll love your shades, there are new products and techniques that can help you save time, money, and energy. And there is a world of beautiful fabrics just quietly waiting for your special touch to turn them into exciting decor.

So get busy! Size up the situation and begin creating your own impressive professional-looking shades.

ENERGY SAVERS

Shades are one of the simplest and most energy efficient window treatments. Used alone or added to an existing window treatment, shades can help you achieve energy benefits in both winter and summer. A shade can help hold heat in in the winter and reflect heat out in the summer months.

To understand further why shades should be considered for your windows it helps to know a little about R-value, which is the degree of resistance to heat flow, including winter heat loss and summer heat gain. An insulated 2x4 stud wall has an R-value of about 10 to 13. A single pane of glass has only a 0.89 R-value. Double glazing yields 1.8, triple glazing 2.8, and quadruple glazing 3.7. It is easy to see that a lot of energy is literally going out the windows.

Even simple shades, carefully constructed and installed can yield a 2.0 R-value, 4.0 can be achieved with quilted types of construction, and some types of Roman shades, sealed at edges and incorporating several layers of fiber batting have been rated from 2.5 to 5.5.

A study by the Illinois Institute of Technology in 1975 revealed the following information. In summer a sunlit window with a shade admits 50% less heat than a bare window. A shade on a non-sunlit window admits 25% less heat. In winter the use of shades in a house with 15% window area reduces heat loss by about 10%. However, when the outside temperature is above 20° the shades should be raised to allow for passive solar heat gain where possible. A shade set inside a casement reduces heat loss by 25%. Hung loosely outside the recess, effectiveness drops to 10%-15%.

3

Another study showed that a good quality opaque (room darkening) shade can cut summer heat gain by 63%; while translucent shades cut heat by 44%.

It is important to remember that these results were obtained in controlled laboratory situations. Your home is not a laboratory. Each room and each window can have variables affecting results. Just how much energy savings you can achieve with your newly constructed shades depends on other factors too, particularly the method of installation, the style or type of shade, the fabric, backing and method of construction used, and whether or not you USE them.

In order to achieve maximum benefit from your shades here are a few guidelines:

SNUG ACCURATE MOUNT
Shades should be mounted to fit snugly without gaps where air can flow around or under them. This means they should fit accurately and snugly on inside mounts and be 'sealed' or snug to the wall on outside mounts. It may mean giving up a fancy hem treatment in favor of energy savings, or adding a cornice to trap air at the top of the window. (For cornice construction ideas see Decorating with Fabric/An Idea Book by Judy Lindahl.)

Roller shades mounted inside with maximum 1/4" clearance on sides will be most effective. Roman Shades with inside mounts are more efficient than conventional outside mounts.

SHADE STYLE AFFECTS ENERGY SAVINGS
The type of shade treatment you select contributes to the energy saved. Roller shades with a straight bottom that can rest on the sill to help 'seal' the treatment will give maximum results when coupled with tight fitting side and top clearance.

Roman shades that fall flat and fit snugly at sides and bottom will be most energy efficient. The goal is to eliminate gaps

4

where air can flow around and under the shade. Folded or pleated types such as hobbled shades, the softly gathered and often sheer cloud shades, and Austrian shades will be the least energy efficient.

Combining shades with other treatments--i.e. drapes, cur-tains, shutters, and other shades can produce additional energy savings.

See ENERGY SAVING DECORATING by Judy Lindahl for more specific details and do-it-yourself information for creating efficient treatments.

METHOD OF CONSTRUCTION
The choice of fabric and lining or backing has a definite affect on the amount of energy saved, too. The tighter the weave, the better. Thus sheers and open weave fabrics will be least efficient. For roller shades the more opaque and dense the backing the more energy saved. Therefore blackout (room darkening) shades save more energy than translucent types.

Dark colors will absorb heat--which may be fine in winter, but not in summer. In some extreme cases dark fabrics could cause enough heat build-up in summer to shatter glass. So as a general rule a lighter color is preferred for a backing fabric on shades. A possible alternative would be reversible, light to dark, shades or one set of shades for each season. (Seasonal decorating is regaining popularity.)

When constructing Roman shades, it is a good idea to select a thermal type of lining fabric whenever possible. Roc Lon is one type that has thermal qualities, yet remains flexible enough that it does not detract from the pleating action of the shade.

Many people have been experimenting with a layer (even up to three layers) of fiberfill, such as Polar Guard[R] manufactured by Celanese, and other types of quilt battings. These add

5

effectively to energy savings, but also add considerably to the bulk of the shade. One inevitably may have to choose for themselves between asthetics and the efficiency of this method.

A thinner layer of Thermolam[R] Plus (by Stacy) or Pellon Fleece also lend insulating value with much less bulk. To improve energy efficiency even further a layer of plastic film (4 mil) can be added under the decorator fabric and on top of the fiber filling.

Perhaps the most promising product for providing maximum insulation with minimum bulk is the needle punch mylar insulating lining beginning to appear in many fabric stores. Developed originally for the outerwear industry, it offers many possibilities for other decorating uses as well. This fabric has fuzzy polyester fibers on both sides with a thin layer of heat reflecting Mylar in the middle. It is light weight, thin and flexible, 45" wide, inexpensive (approx. $2.00 yd.), and easy to work with. Be on the alert for it.

In shade construction fiber layers should be cut the finished size of the shade and inserted into the shade construction between the decorator fabric and lining. Because of the additional bulk they create, you will need to allow more fabric for side hems on your shade to compensate. Try making a small sample by wrapping a piece of decorator fabric around the edge of your layers of insulation to judge the added length needed.

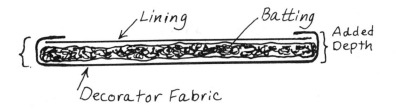

It is important that the shade fit snugly in the window opening. Some designers suggest making the padded, insulated Roman shades 1/2" to 1" wider than the opening to assure a snug fit.

The bulk of added insulating layers will also create a need for additional length in the shade fabric which will be taken up if you are sewing tucks or folds. To get an idea of how much length is needed for each tuck, make a sample including fabric, batting, lining, and inserting slat or dowel if called for. Release the tuck and measure it. Then add the appropriate amount for each tuck on your shade style.

Another modification you may wish to make is to place the weight bar at the hem edge, rather than in a pocket higher up on the shade.

TIME SAVERS

There are some general techniques and equipment that can help to minimize the time and energy you expend. These are the sanity savers that keep do-it-yourselfers forging ahead.

GRAPHING

Drawing a miniature finished version of your shade, especially Roman shade types, is a terrific time saver in the end. You can locate mounting ease, ring and pleat location, hem location and depth, rod pocket placement, slat placement, seams, splices, etc. It helps you think through the project, making it less likely for you to commit errors. It does not have to be perfect and to scale, but all the necessary numbers should be there.

Be sure to make any notes or comments to yourself right on your sketch. Then you won't forget them later.

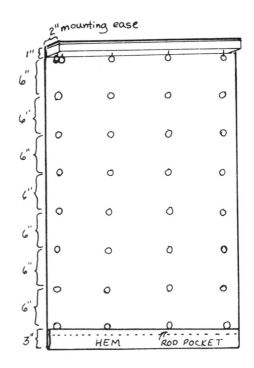

FOLDING CARDBOARD CUTTING BOARD

These are available in fabric stores and fabric departments. Easiest to use are the type with a 1" ruled grid.

The cutting board makes life much easier when you use it to square your fabric, backing or lining. Mark the positions for pleats, tucks, rings, or slats. You can pin into it, and press on it.

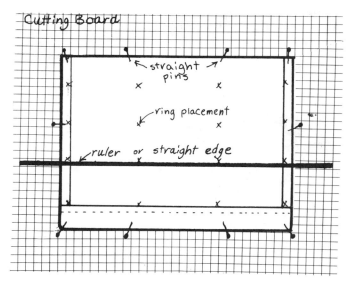

For large shades use two boards pushed together, or cut a second one in half and tape to the first.

Your work surface should be large enough to support the entire shade. This means more accuracy in measuring and cutting, and reduces the amount that the fabric must be handled. A 4' x 8' sheet of plywood, a ping pong table, several tables pushed together in a recreation hall or church basement may all work. Least desirable is to crawl around on the floor (it's terribly hard on knees and back), but it can be done if necessary.

EXTENDING YOUR CARPENTER'S SQUARE

One of the most important tools in decorating is the carpenter's square, available in hardware departments.

It is indespensible for accurate cor- ners--especially if you are not using a cutting board graph. Because the sides on the carpenter's square are quite short, it becomes difficult to achieve accuracy on long edges. One solution is to extend the square by slipping on a piece of aluminum U-channel available in hardware departments and stores. The channel just fits the size of the square. It is available in 6' and 8' lengths and provides a good smooth straight edge.

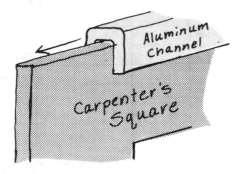

METAL STRAIGHT EDGE GUIDES

In shade making a long straight edge for marking is often more important than ruled markings. One inch by eighth-inch aluminum flat bar in 6' or 8' lengths solves this prob-lem nicely. It is available in hardware stores and is much less expensive than metal rulers. An old Venetian blind slat makes a nice alternative when you can get one.

DECORATOR STRAIGHT PINS

Actually these are 1-1/4" or 1-1/2" corsage pins available from floral supply or hobby and craft shops. They make the best all around sewing pins. Their extra length makes it fast and easy to secure layers of fabric, tucks, and pleats. The glass ball head makes them easy to hold and to locate.

GLUING

The use of tacky fast-drying fabric glues like Wilhold, Quik, Super Tacky, Fab Trim, or the roller shade laminating glues can short-cut many steps in shade making. For example
- Glue trims to shades
- Glue up a facing or hem
- Glue on a ring tape, then stitch it
- Glue -treat edges of fabric to prevent fraying
- Glue-treat knots so they won't slip or untie

FUSING

When gluing won't work or isn't practical, fusing may be the answer. Stacy's Stitch Witchery® Pellon Sav-A-Stitch, Poly Web, Perky Bond are just some of the many available brands.

Fusible webs are monofilaments of extremely heat sensitive fiber arranged in a random pattern. They are available by the yard in most fabric stores and fabric departments. They come in 18" widths and in pre-cut strips and rolls.

How Do They Work?

The webbing is placed between two layers of fabric, heat is applied, the webbing melts, and the two fabrics are effectively fused or 'bonded' together. You might think of it as a dry glue that is activated by heat.

Always read and follow the directions that come with the webbing! They will indicate the need to use HEAT, MOISTURE, and PRESSURE. I like to add PATIENCE.
1. Heat - from your iron, usually a wool, steam setting.
2. Moisture - from the steam iron PLUS a damp press cloth.
3. PRESSure - NOT a sliding, ironing motion. Use an up/down motion. This enables adequate heat to de- velop to melt the webbing, and prevent stretching

the fabric.

4. Time - Your iron must be placed in each position for a length of time--usually 10 to 15 seconds--to create enough heat for the web to melt and BOND completely. This takes...

5. Patience! But the reward is a beautiful bond with no stitches. Improper bonds may loosen in washing or cleaning, so it is worth the effort to do it right the first time. Resist the urge to peek and peel the fabric to see if the bond is taking. The bond sets as it cools.

Yes, all of us will occasionally get some of the fusible on our irons. Easiest way to clean it off is to use one of the hot iron cleaners (Clean and Glide by Stacy or Dritz Iron-Off) that you will find in the notions department.

Where To Use Fusible Web

- For hemming
- To fuse seam allowances or side hems , then turn them and stitch. You can then insert weight rods, slats, etc. without 'hanging up" in the seam or hem.

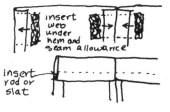

- Attach appliques, ribbons, trims, etc.
  Note: If you fuse trim first on Roman-type shades, then stitch it, it will not shift, creep, or crawl.
- To stiffen and strengthen fabric in hems and comices.
- To make roller shades. See pp. 30-31.

WATER SOLUBLE MARKERS

These new marking pens, examples include Wonder Marker and Mark B Gone™ by Dritz ᴿ, are perfect for marking hems, locations for rings, trims, pleats, tucks, etc. You just draw right on the fabric, then rub gently with a well moistened cloth to remove the marks. Always test the marker on a scrap of fabric. Pens can be found in notions departments.

FRAY CHECK

Dritz Fray Check™ is a clear liquid that can be applied to edges of fabrics to prevent raveling. You may find it to be easier to use than the bead of glue method described later in this book. Always try a test sample on your fabric scrap before proceeding with the whole project. Look for Fray Check in notions departments.

DOFF T-RINGS

This new product allows Roman shade rings to be applied with no sewing. Clear plastic ring has a T-stem extension. The rings are applied using a tool much like those used in department stores to attach the plastic fasteners that hold price tags, etc. The 'T' portion remains on the right side of the shade and is least conspicuous on white or light colored fabrics, and completely inconspicuous on most prints or gathered shades (i.e. cloud). Shank length is standard causing looser fit on thin shades and snugger fit on energy types.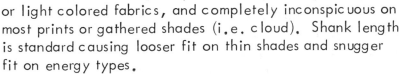

SHIRRING AND SMOCKING TAPES

Gathered or smocked shade and valance headings are simplified with the new polyester Gosling Tapes from Europe. Tapes are sewn flat, then woven-in pulling cords are drawn up, creating a shirred or smocked style. The polyester tapes are washable and cleanable and do not shrink. They are nearly invisible from the outside. The traditional cotton 2 and 4-cord shirring tapes may also be used. These tapes require more lines of stitching but create a distinctive look of their own for decorative shade or valance headings.

ROLLER SHADES

I n the following pages you will find a variety of methods for creating roller shades. All methods may not work on every fabric. The lighter fabrics will require heavier, sturdier backing. Some methods require no backing at all.

The cost of construction will vary with different methods as will the appearance--mainly from the street side. Non-backed single-layer shades show more color to the outside while backed methods are more opaque and allow no light or color at all if constructed from a black-out or room-darkening backing. Since some people love lots of color from outside and others prefer a more uniform look, this is definitely a consideration in choosing a method.

With construction affecting finished product, it is very advisable to make a test sample of methods you are considering. If this is not possible, try to look at shades made from fabric similar to the type you are considering.

ANATOMY OF A SHADE

The terms and parts for roller shades are few, but a basic background is helpful. The roller is quite simple and has changed very little since it was invented in 1864 by Stewart Hartshorn. A spring is set into the roller and catches a notched wheel as the shade is adjusted at the window.

Rollers come in three types--wood, cardboard, and steel. You can staple shades to wood or cardboard, and can use tape on all types. (Use only 1/4" or 3/16" staples.)

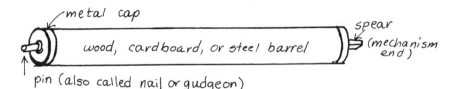

The window width is related to the size of roller diameter. As a shade gets wider, the diameter of the roller increases to assure strength and resistance to sagging. The diameter of the roller will vary from 15/16" for 37" to 1-1/4" for 80" rollers in wood and cardboard. Steel rollers range from 1" for 37" shades to 3" for 7' to 15' shades.

If your shade will be heavier than average, as in a laminated shade, it will be best to select a heavy duty roller. A very long shade will also require a heavy duty roller. The added expense is slight; the benefits are well worth it.

Shortening of a roller is always done from <u>pin</u> end to avoid disturbing the roller spring mechanism.

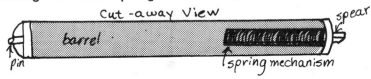

To cut a roller down to window size, remove the pin with pliers, and pull off the metal cap. Saw roller to size, replace the cap, and hammer the pin into place. Be sure the pin goes in <u>straight.</u>

You will want to be familiar with the three widths illustrated below. Keep in mind that for installation purposes rollers are always measured from <u>tip-to-tip.</u>

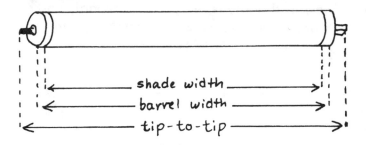

shade width

barrel width

tip-to-tip

Bare rollers can be purchased cut-to-fit from shade shops and often in hardware or variety and some mail order stores. If necessary, you can purchase an inexpensive ready-made shade and remove the plastic and use its roller and slat. The basic danger of this is that the inexpensive roller may not have a spring of good enough quality to lift the weight of a fabric shade. If you do choose this method, re-cycle the plastic shade by using it for a pattern, then as a drop cloth for painting or arts and crafts projects.

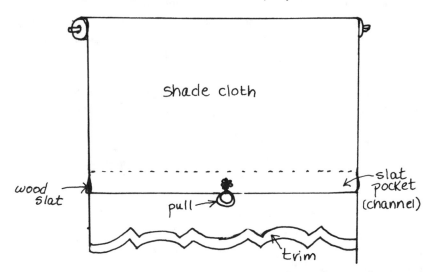

shade cloth

wood slat

pull

slat pocket (channel)

trim

The wooden slat across the bottom of a shade is not necessary, but helps the shade hold its shape and prevents the sides from curling. Slats need about a 1-1/4" tuck which can be on the front or back side of the shade. The channel or tuck should be at least 2" above the top of the decorative edge, if one is used.

16

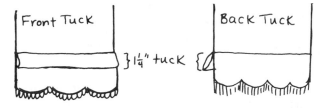

Front Tuck   }1¼" tuck{   Back Tuck

MOUNTING

Roller shades are mounted in one of two ways--reverse roll or conventional roll. In either case it is the same roller. It is just a matter of positioning the spear and the way the shade is mounted on the roller that makes the difference.

REVERSE ROLL

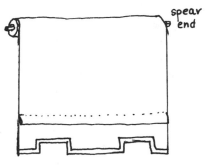

spear end

The spear (flat) end should be on your right when the fabric side of the shade faces you. The shade cloth is in front of the roller causing the shade to sit out from the window a bit. This method avoids handles or projections, the roller does not show, but streaks of light are more likely along the edges of the shade in some window types.

CONVENTIONAL ROLL

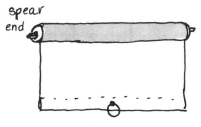

spear end

The spear is on your left. The shade fabric comes off the back of the shade causing the shade to fit closer to the window. This prevents light streaks and gives more energy savings. The roller will show unless a cornice or valance is used.

MEASURING

I t is extremely important that you take accurate measurements for your shades. An inaccuracy of even 1/4"
can prevent smooth action and fit. Cloth tape meas-
ures or strings can stretch, so use a wood rule or metal tape.

Windows may look the same size, but seldom are. Frames will
often vary slightly from top to bottom and from one window to
another. For this reason be sure to measure each window sepa-
rately at the point where the brackets will be installed.

There are many styles of brackets for different purposes and
window types. (Be sure to read Directory of Shade Brackets
pp. 58-62. In addition there are heavy duty and extension
brackets in most styles to accommodate long, heavy, or
thick shades. The longer a shade is, or the more textured
the fabric is, the "fatter" it gets on the roller. This may
require the use of heavy duty or extension brackets to allow for the extra weight and space. It will usually also call
for the heavy duty roller mentioned earlier. (Four to five
feet in length is about maximum in a laminated shade for
a regular roller.)

WIDTH

Mark the position where the brackets are to be installed.
Be sure the marks, and hence the brackets, are level or
the shade may not roll.

Since the actual diameter of roller plus shade will not be
known until the shade is complete, you may wish to mark
bracket positions and wait to install them until the shade
is finished.

Inside Brackets

Measure from one inside surface of the window frame to the opposite inside surface. In other words "wood to wood." If your roller is being cut for you, indicate this is tip-to-tip measurement for an IBM (inside bracket mount); thus the dealer will automatially subtract 1/8" for clearance in the window. If brackets are already mounted and you are cutting your own roller, be sure you measure "wood to wood" and subtract 1/8" to obtain the proper tip-to-tip measurement.

Outside Brackets

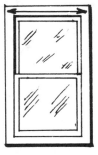

Mark the position of the brackets on trim or wall and measure distance between. Mount brackets so there will be 1-1/2" to 2" of overlap on the window frame. This helps to prevent light streaks along the sides of the shade. When measuring for outside brackets, remember there is a difference between the bracket foot and the bracket. This can affect the fit of the roller.

Bracket Foot – this is mounting position, NOT bracket measuring point.

Bracket! – measure from here

LENGTH

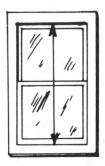

Measure the window opening from top of opening to lower sill and add 12" to 16" roll-over. This is the safety margin left on the roller when the shade is pulled down. It prevents the shade from being torn from the roller when the shade is pulled. Twelve inches is standard roll-over. Sixteen is used if the hem is cut into a deep ornamental shape.

CEILING BRACKETS

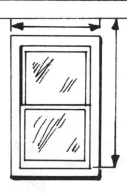

Mark position where brackets will be placed and measure the distance between. It is recommended that the shade overlap the window frame 1-1/2" to 2". For the length measure from the ceiling to the lower window sill.

BOTTOM-UP INSTALLATION

Measure the same as for inside or outside brackets, but take measurements at bottom of window opening. If brackets are installed on sill or floor, mark the position where the brackets will be positioned and measure distance between them.

REPLACING OLD SHADES

If you are replacing the entire shade, roller too, measurements are taken as described above. If you are replacing only the shade cloth, measure the shade fabric, if it fits and hangs well.

STEP ONE: GET READY

I. CHOOSE SHADE FABRIC

Firmly woven fabric is important, especially for larger shades. Looser weaves will tend to stretch and ravel more easily. Fabric may be placed on the crosswise direction, design permitting, since it will be stabilized when fused, bonded, or glued. This will allow wider shades than the normal fabric width of 45" or 54", with no splices. It is a helpful trick for short but wide ranch style windows.

2. MAKE A TEST SAMPLE

Select the methods you feel are best for your fabric and the placement of the shade. Try them according to the detailed instructions in the following section on Making the Shade. Evaluate them and make a selection.

The following questions may also help in the decision:
- Is the method compatible with the fabric to produce enough but not too much body? If backing is too light weight, the edges of the shade ripple. The shade may not have body to maintain shape. Liquid stiffeners often don't "take" on fabrics treated with Scotchguard or ZePel type products.
- Is room darkening desired? Only commercial blackout backings can provide complete darkening. Some methods are more translucent than others. Hold samples up to light to check for coloration changes and light transmission.
- What about sun fading? Some fading can be expected over a period of time. Bright and dark colors are most susceptable. The laminated shades are most protected. Light colors fade least.
- How much am I willing or able to spend? No matter what method you choose, you will be saving 40% to 60% (or more) over a custom shade.
- What is available in my area? Not all backings or stiffeners are available everywhere, so having a variety of choices is an advantage. Fusible webs and drapery linings are found in most fabric shops and can often be mail ordered. Commercial backings are available from shade shops and

by mail from some companies. Stiffeners and sprays are usually found in fabric stores and drapery or shade shops, and by catalog.

3. ASSEMBLE MATERIALS

Roller	Backing or Stiffener
Brackets	Staple gun or Tape
Fabric	Carpenter's square
Slat	Cardboard cutting board
Shade Pull	Scissors
Trim	Straight Edge Guides
Rulers	Glue or Fray Check
Iron	Press cloth

Note: Just a reminder about the importance of a large work surface. A shade hanging over the edge of an ironing board or table can easily be stretched or distorted, and it is difficult to keep measurements and marking accurate.

4. CUTTING TO GENERAL SIZE

Cut the fabric (and backing if one is used) one to two inches wider--approximately the tip-to-tip measurement of the roller, and one to two inches longer than finished cut dimensions. Remember the length includes 12" to 16" for rollover. The shade will be trimmed to the exact measurements later.

Be sure to cut sharp clean edges with no ravelings. Strings or ravelings that get between the fabric and backing during the bonding process will show through as dark lines when a translucent shade is hung in the window.

If your fabric requires splicing, you will be preparing the cut edges of the splices at this time, too. Be sure to read through the section on Splicing Pointers pp. 35-38.

Take your time as you lay out your fabric. Be sure you

have design motifs centered where they look their best.
Take care in laying out pieces that will be spliced. Care
now pays dividends later.

STEP TWO: MAKING THE SHADE — A VARIETY OF CONSTRUCTION METHODS

IRON-ON BACKINGS

The development of these backings has made do-it-yourself shade making easier and very professional. Iron-ons require heat and pressure to activate the adhesive and insure a good bond.

Woven iron-on backings include Tran Lam (translucent), Tri Lam (blackout), Bond Lam (translucent), etc. They are generally available in 36", 45", and 68" widths. Wider widths may sometimes be special ordered in shade shops.

NOTE: These backings may be used lengthwise (A) or crosswise (B) in a window. However, they are best used CROSSWISE whenever possible, as the shade will roll better and smoother especially in REVERSE ROLL. If heavy fabrics do create puckers when rolled in reverse, use a conventional roll and add a cornice or valance if you wish to hide the roller.

selvage   (A)   selvage   (B)

Lengthwise   Crosswise

crosswise   Lengthwise

Bonding Woven Iron-on Backing

1. Cut fabric and backing to general size (See p. 22) and mark center top and bottom. Place the backing on the padded work surface and remove paper liner which protects the adhesive. Set the liner aside and save.

24

2. Center the fabric on top of the adhesive and smooth in place with your hands to remove air bubbles.

3. Using a cool DRY iron, press fabric from center outward. Once the fabric has been pressed in place with a cool iron, turn the iron up to the fabric temperature and continue ironing with short, slow, smooth strokes.

Let cool completely. The bond sets as the fabric cools. NEVER TOUCH THE BACK- ING WITH A HOT IRON. If you do press on the backing side, as with heavier fabrics or when making a slat pocket, use the paper liner as a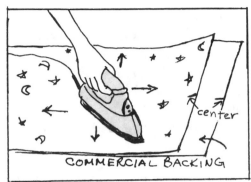

COMMERCIAL BACKING

"press-cloth" and place it on top of the backing before using the iron.

The amount of pressing each fabric requires will vary. Light weights take less time and heat, heavy weights take more. Heavy weights usually also require pressing from both front (let the fabric cool before you turn it) and back sides to assure a good bond.

While these backing fabrics give very professional results, the products tend to come and go from the market. When they cannot be found, laminating fabric to commercial shade material with laminating glue is the next best option, especially if you desire a blackout shade. Using laminating glue is quite easy, and you can glue fabric to shades you already have, as well as purchasing separate backing material.

NON-WOVEN FUSIBLE BACKINGS

Style-A-Shade™ by Stacy is perhaps the backing most readily available at this time. Other fusible interfacings may be considered, but it is always advisable to make a test sample and be sure to follow manufacturer's directions for fusing.

Style-A-Shade™ is a washable, cleanable fusible which bonds easily to fabrics and is not discolored by sunlight. Its limiting factors can be width (now in 45") which could necessitate splicing, and the fact that it is not as opaque as might be desirable to give a white uniform appearance to the outside of the house. The manufacturer also suggests it is not recommended for very light weight fabrics or sheers.

It is a good idea to request the backing be rolled rather than folded when you purchase it. Even though the folds will probably press out in the fusing process, it will be easier to handle and to splice if it is kept smooth.

Sometimes with heavier fabrics non-woven backings roll well in conventional roll, but pucker if reverse rolled. It is wise to test roll your sample.

Note: I have found that many non-wovens (including Style-A-Shade) roll more smoothly and evenly in a crosswise direction. This means splices will then occur horizontally, which is desirable. See splicing pointers on pp. 35-38.

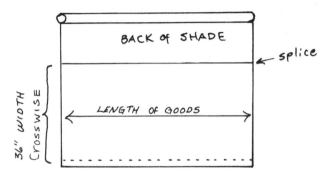

26

To Bond Style-A-Shade™

Place the Style-A-Shade™ on the padded work surface with fusible up. Position fabric carefully on top. Use 'wool' steam setting and a damp press cloth.

Start in the center and work out to the sides. Press for 10-15 seconds over entire area. Use an up and down pressing motion. Do not slide the iron. Let cool to room temperature then turn over and repeat on other side.

If the backing must be spliced, place fabric down on work surface first, then place the backing pieces on top, butting or barely overlapping the smooth cut edges carefully together.

Use a see-thru press cloth so that you will be able to see that the splice is accurate.

GLUING TO A SHADE OR BACKING

This is a relatively easy process and almost the only way to obtain an energy efficient room darkening shade. In this method laminating glue is rolled onto the shade with a paint roller, and then the decorative fabric is smoothed into place.

There are several approaches with this method:
1. You can purchase backing by the yard from a shade shop then measure, cut and laminate it yourself.
2. If you already have a good quality vinyl or cloth shade, you can laminate your fabric to it.
3. You can purchase a good quality plain shade and glue the fabric to it.

If your shade comes with the slat at the bottom edge you may use it that way. For a different look, you can cut the slat off, then move the slat tuck higher up on the shade, leaving room for a decorative edge. (See Shade Trim Ideas.)

If you purchase your plain shade through a shade shop, you might have them sew the tuck where you want it and leave a plain bottom edge. You can then cut your own design and glue trim to the edge to complete the shade.

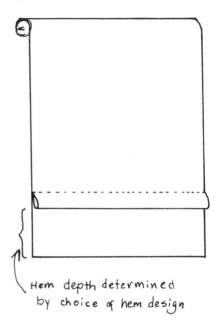

Hem depth determined by choice of hem design

The best results will be obtained with a medium to heavy vinyl coated shade cloth. While it is <u>possible</u> to glue to a very inexpensive plastic shade, you will nearly always get puckers on the back side. This is partly due to the light weight plastic and to the fact that you can't use an iron to help set and smooth the laminating process.

It is best to use a commercial laminating glue (such as Graber Laminating Adhesive or Lamashade) available in quart or gallon sizes through shade shops or drapery departments. These glues dry clear and FLEXIBLE. If you cannot locate a commercial glue, a craft glue (Wilhold, Quik) may work. Test it first by pouring a small amount on a piece of fabric. If it dries clear and flexible, it is a possibility. Then make a sample with fabric and shade backing, or high up on your roller shade. I have used Sobo on occasion with reasonable success, but Elmer's seems unacceptable as it dries hard and too stiff.

Bonding with Laminating Adhesive

1. Cover the unpadded work surface with brown paper or heavy plastic. Masking tape all the edges of the backing which has been pre-cut to general size (see p. 22), fastening one edge along the edge of the table. This serves as a guideline for a straight edge.
2. Center the fabric over the backing, then tape the top edge in place about 1" above the backing. (If you are working on a ready-made shade, tape the fabric just below the roller.

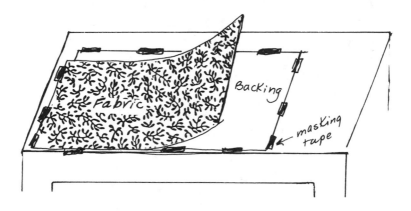

3. Now carefully roll the fabric up on a tube, keeping the edge along the table straight and even. To start bring the fabric back over the tube until side edges line up. Then roll all the way to the masking tape.

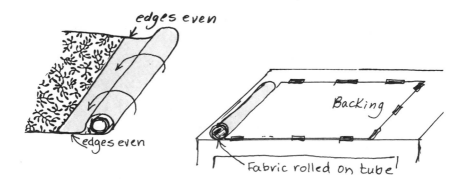

4. Pour glue into a paint roller pan, then thoroughly coat a short nap or sponge roller. Now roll quickly and evenly until a thin coat of glue covers every single inch of the backing. There must be no skips or dry areas. If the glue is applied too thick, it may come through to the front when fabric is applied.

NOTE: Glue sets up faster in hot weather, so try to glue in the cool of the morning.

5. Begin to roll the fabric slowly and evenly onto the backing, smoothing with your hands as you go. (Always work WITH stripes, not across them.) Then take a medium warm iron and go over the whole shade, slowly and evenly. This helps to start the glue drying and removes air pockets, assuring a good bond. Allow the glue to dry overnight if possible (at least 8 hours) before cutting and shaping.

Clean up glue with water immediately after finishing. Glue is water soluble while wet, but permanent when dry. Wear old clothes. If you need to carry over the gluing to another day, wrap the paint roller in plastic and put it in the refrigerator. It will keep for well over a week this way.

NOTE: Be sure to read Splicing Pointers for face fabric splicing details.

FUSIBLE WEBBING WITH FABRIC BACKING

This method involves the heat sensitive webbings described earlier in Time Savers. It makes a durable and very attractive shade though it takes more time and patience to construct. Materials are readily available in fabric stores, and the shades always roll well in conventional or reverse.

1. Make a "sandwich" of the face fabric and cotton sateen drapery lining (or firmly woven white fabric) with the fusible web in the middle. The web will need to be overlapped to create enough width, as it is only 18" wide.

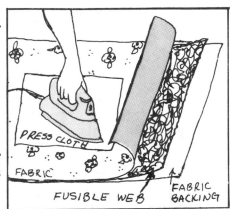

wrong side of fabric

fusible web

fabric backing

2. Follow directions for applying the webbing carefully--including the use of adequate amounts of heat, moisture, and pressure (NOT IRONING). It is advisable to use a damp press cloth in the process. This protects the fabric and gives more intense heat and steam.

PRESS CLOTH

FABRIC

FUSIBLE WEB

FABRIC BACKING

3. Start in the center and press your way out to the sides. Be careful not to lift or pull the fabric while it is warm or push the iron (ironing motion) hard on the fabric. This can stretch edges and cause distortion that may prevent the shade from looking attractive and hanging correctly. Be sure to steam press from both sides, allowing the fabric to cool before turning it.

LIQUID STIFFENERS AND AEROSOL SPRAYS

These methods have no backing. The fabric itself is stiffened. No backing means a 'thinner' shade when it is rolled up, thus longer shades are possible. Color will show outside the house and sun fading may be a problem. Bold graphic designs of 100% cotton often put on stretcher bars are good in this method. If splicing is required there is no choice but to sew a seam or fuse an overlap. The stiffeners I am aware of are Graber Fabric Stiffener and Baco--imported from England by Conran's in New York. You might try a very dilute white glue solution or go heavy on the liquid starch.

Aerosol Spray Stiffeners

Two commercial products, Make-A-Shade and Kwik-Shade are aerosol sprays which will stiffen fabrics. Hang the pressed fabric from a rafter in a well ventilated area, and spray from both sides. When fabric is dry and stiff, proceed with cutting and mounting. As with all methods, a test sample is recommended. (A clear acrylic spray will give similar results.)

ADDITIONAL SHADE IDEAS

FREE HANGING FABRIC

A simple and easy way to attach fabric for use with an old shade is to staple or tape the fabric to the roller so it hangs

free on top of the old shade. This is particu-larly good if you have a room darkening shade you wish to use. Cut the fabric just slightly wider than the old shade. (You may want to starch the fabric for more body by laying it on a flat sur-face and sponging on un-diluted liquid starch and letting it dry, or use one of the commercial stiffen-ings listed previously.)

Staple fabric to roller; put the shade in the window and check for straight rolling. If the fabric and shade should not roll

32

compatibly, you can use the fabric alone or bond it to a backing. If the two roll well together, proceed and add a slat pocket, treat edges for raveling. Each can have a slat, and the fabric can have a shaped and trimmed hem if desired. The pull should be underneath on the old shade.

TRIM A SHADE

A very easy way to give an inexpensive shade a new look is to cut off the old slat hem......

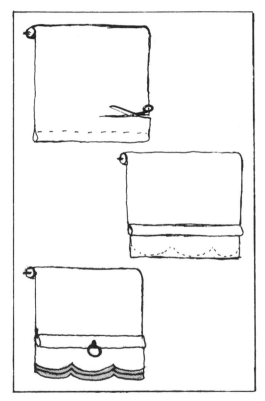

sew a new one higher up, trace on a new decorative hem treatment......

cut the new hem, glue on one or two rows of trim, add a shade pull....and your shade has a new look!!!

This is effective to tie the shade together with room color scheme or draperies. Also good in damp steamy shower or tub areas where an all fabric shade might be affected by moisture. If shade will be hung in damp area--preshrinking the trim before applying it is strongly advised.

CONTRASTING HEM

A good way to tie cornice and shade together for a special effect is to use a contrasting hem section. That is, make the cornice (or valance) from one fabric and the body of the shade from a second. Try reverse ground prints, print mix coordinates, stripes and dots, solids and prints, etc. This is an attractive shade and practical too, if you don't have quite enough of one fabric to do the whole shade.

Bond shade according to your chosen method. Splice on last 7"-8" in contrasting fabric. (Review the next chapter on Splicing Pointers)

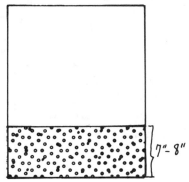

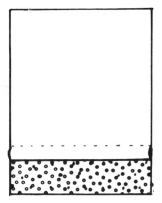

Sew or fuse the slat pocket, positioning it so the splice line is underneath the pocket where it will not show.

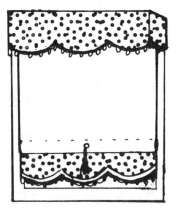

Finish the shade, adding slat, trim and pull. Make the coordinating cornice or valance.

34

SPLICING POINTERS

On occasion you will find your backing or face fabric will
not be long enough or wide enough, and you will have to
make a splice. THINK the problem through first. Chances
are you can conceal the splice with some good planning.

BACKING SPLICES

If you are making a shade with a fabric backing such as drapery lining, it may be necessary to splice it in order to make
a shade wider than the standard 45" width of the fabric. For
backings, always position the splice on
the crosswise, NOT lengthwise direction.
This prevents any posibility of a streak
running the full length of the translucent
shade.

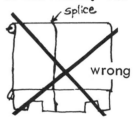

Then think out the position of the splice
even further. Plan so it falls--

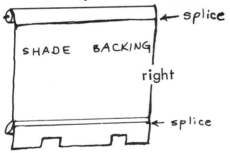

(1) high on the shade where
it will be rolled out of
sight most of the time

and/or

(2) low on the shade where
it will be in or behind
the slat pocket.

A little pre-planning can eliminate a lot of problems.
It is very important that the two edges of the splice meet
and overlap <u>very slightly</u>, about 1/16" - 1/8". This prevents a "dimple" or ridge on the right side of the shade.
This dimple, if it occurs, cannot be removed by pressing.

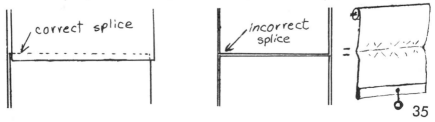

FACE FABRIC SPLICES

When you have to splice a face fabric, the best choice of backings would be 1) a commercial backing (blackout if possible), or 2) a fusible web method. Also decide whether you might be able to turn the fabric on the crosswise and position the splice high on the shade, or behind the slat pocket. Remember sheets are often wide enough not to require splicing.

When a face fabric is spliced, it is handled in the same manner as you would a bedspread or round tablecloth. The 'seam' is not placed down the middle, but is centered equally toward the edges of the shade.

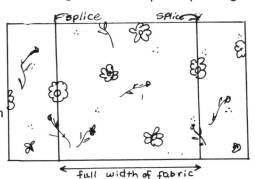

To achieve a good splice cut the fabric edges with smooth clean strokes using very sharp scissors, making sure the patterns match.

Preparing Fabric For Splicing
Here is a step–by–step method for preparing fabric edges that must be spliced and butted together.

Prepare and lay out center panel and side pieces with fabric cut and ready for exact matching of the design.

Fold under the edge on one side piece until it matches the design of the center panel. Mark the center panel lightly, then cut off the excess fabric. Repeat on the other side.

36

Now place the cut edge on top of the side panel, taking care to match the design accurately. Using the cut edge as your guide carefully cut through the lower layer to remove the excess fabric.

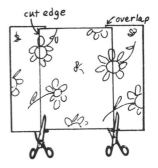

This now leaves clean cut edges that can be butted to-gether into a carefully match-ed splice.

Note: Be sure there are no ravellings or strings that could get trapped under the fabric when it is spliced.

Iron-On Splices
Draw a guide line for the center panel and press it into place first. Then proceed with side panels.

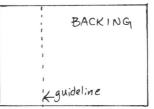

Position the edges carefully on the backing making sure they come evenly together before you press. Be careful to prevent stretching the edges as you work. Use an up/down motion of the iron.

Glued Splices
For glued shades follow the general directions with the fol-lowing adjustments. Draw a guideline for center panel placement.

Prepare three tubes for rolling fabric. One tube for the center panel and two shorter ones for the sides.

Tape center panel in place.
Roll it back out of the way.
Roll the side splices carefully onto short tubes. Roll
glue on backing. Gently
roll out the center panel
aligning cut edge to guide
line. Roll each side section
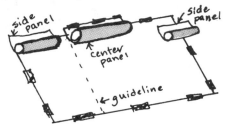
into place carefully matching the pattern as you go. Smooth with hands, iron, let dry and continue with shade.

EXTENDING LENGTH

If you are working with a limited length of fabric and need a longer shade, one answer I have used is to splice on an exten-sion which would be in the 'roll-over' area or would be cov-ered by a valance or cornice.

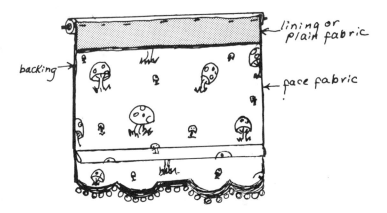

Also see directions for 'Contrasting Hem' on page 34.

STEP THREE: THE FINISHING TOUCHES

The finished width of your shade is usually determined as
follows:

    Inside Brackets: Shade cloth can often be as wide as, or
                slightly wider than the barrel of the roller.
                Just so it does not rub and fray on brackets.

    Outside Brackets: Usually 1/8" to 1/4" from barrel ends to
                prevent rubbing on brackets.

    Sash-run Bracket: 1/4" to 1/2" from barrel ends to prevent
                rubbing on brackets or window molding.

Be as accurate as possible. Improperly measured and trimmed shades may roll off center or not roll at all. Use your
cardboard cutting board and carpenter's square for accurate
90° angles and straight edges.

I. Mark the long edges of the shade first using a long
    straight edge. Place the guide along one edge of the
    shade and line it up according to design or grain line.
    Using tailor's chalk or pencil, mark lightly. Then re-
    position the guide along the other long edge. (Take
    measurements at several points to be sure the two edges
    have been marked exactly parallel to one another if you
    have not been using a cutting board graph.)

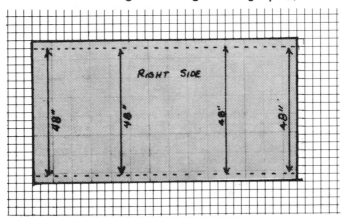

2. Carefully square and mark the short ends. (If you are not using a cutting board graph, be sure to use a carpenter's square for this step.

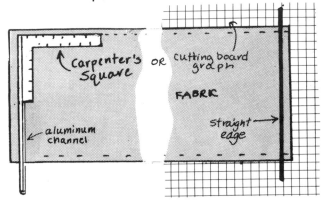

3. Carefully cut along the marked lines with SHARP scissors, using long smooth strokes. Try not to lift or handle the fabric edges any more than necessary.

4. While the fabric is still flat on the work surface, slide it over to the edge of the table so that it just barely extends over the edge. To prevent edges from ravelling run a little white craft or laminating glue along the edge. Put a little glue on your finger, then draw the glue along the edge of the fabric, just barely touching it and leaving a small trail behind. Pat the edge gently and Wipe off any excess glue as you go. Treat top and sides. Let one dry before moving on to the next.

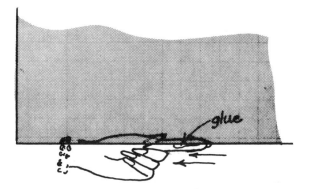

5. The slat pocket can be sewn, glued, or bonded. If your sewing machine will not handle the bulk, or if your shade is very wide, it may be worth your while to have a shade shop or upholstery shop stitch the pocket for you. Use long basting stitches to prevent cutting the fabric and be sure the tuck is STRAIGHT. A crooked tuck makes the shade look crooked in the window.

Plain Hem Edge

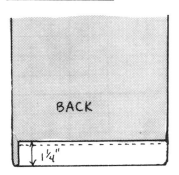

Shaped Hem Edge

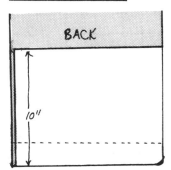

Turn a 1-1/4" tuck to the back side of the shade. Stitch.

Turn a 10" hem to the back side of the shade. Stitch a 1-1/4" tuck.

For Iron-On Backings:

Plain Hem Edge
Cut a 2" strip of backing. Using the paper liner as a press cloth, bond the strip so it covers the fabric and makes a slat pocket.

Shaped Hem Edge
1. Draw two parallel lines 3" apart and 7" to 8" up from bottom of shade.

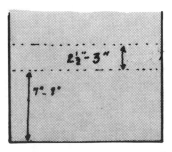

2. Use a press cloth and warm the backing with the iron, then join the lines and press in the tuck.

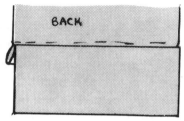

3. Press a 1-1/2" strip of backing across the tuck. Keep the strip even and use a press cloth.

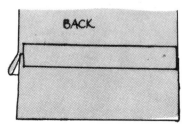

6. If you are using a shaped decorative hem edge, you have probably already selected the design--either one of your own or one from the chapter on Shade Trim Ideas on p. 43. For further ideas look around you for guidelines in the room: the architectural features, the furnishings, etc. Arches and curves may be indicated. Is the room masculine or feminine in character? Look at the fabric itself. The design may suggest scallops, peaks, notched or looped treatment. Try to achieve a shade that will be in harmony with the room and its decor.

Once the design is selected, make a paper pattern. For scallops and curves use plates, saucers, platters, curved sewing rulers, etc. It is often easier to fold a paper strip in half and work out the design.
Make the strip 6" to 10" deep and the width of your shade. Try several ideas until you are satisfied with one.

Cut out the design and open out the paper. You will now have a balanced design.

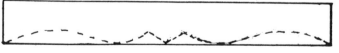

Place the pattern on the shade and weight it or clip it in place so it won't move around. Trace the design onto the shade, then cut it out with sharp scissors.

7. One or more rows of trim may be added to any shade style. Thick gimp or fringe should be glued with decorator craft glue or laminating adhesive. In general gluing is the fastest and easiest way to apply trim.

Run a bead of glue along the position of the trim, then gently press the trim in place. To help maintain sharp clean looking corners and peaks, pinch the trim between your fingers creating a raised area which can be flattened down once the glue has dried.

8. If your roller doesn't have a guideline on it, make one by

holding the roller down firmly on a newspaper on a table or floor. Draw a line smoothly with a felt pen or a piece of chalk.

Using the guideline center your shade and attach it to the roller with tape or 1/4" staples. Be sure you have the roller positioned correctly for reverse or conventional roll.

Reverse Roll   Conventional Roll

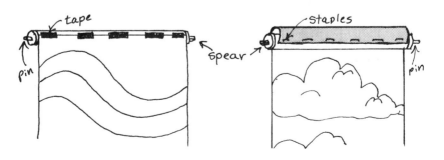

It is very important to attach the shade straight and smooth on the roller. To test for a straight roll pick the shade up off the table and roll it gently onto the roller. (If you try to roll it by pushing it along on the table you can often push it off center.) Then try it at the window in the brackets. If the shade rolls off center---

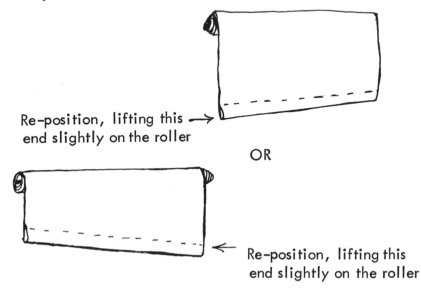

Re-position, lifting this ⟶
end slightly on the roller

OR

Re-position, lifting this
end slightly on the roller

Other reasons your shade may not roll straight:
• Brackets are not level
• Window is out of square
• Shade was not cut on square

9. Add a shade pull. This not only helps keep soiling to a minimum by keeping fingers off the shade, it encourages you to pull the shade in the CENTER, the proper way to keep it on track and rolling straight.
Pulls are available from shade shops, variety stores, home improvement centers, etc. Or you may make your own from macrame, stained glass, drapery rings, pottery.

IMPORTANT INFORMATION

Here are just a few reminders and special points that may help to answer some questions.

SPRING TENSION

Do not twist or attempt to adjust the spear (mechanism end) when the roller is not in its brackets. To adjust a too tight or too loose spring, see directions in Easy Care and Upkeep. However, if a spear should get bumped and the tension is released on the spring, you have probably disengaged the teeth from notch (see Spearlining diagram p. 47. To rewind the spring slip the spear through the tines of a fork, hold the roller firmly and rotate the fork several revolutions.

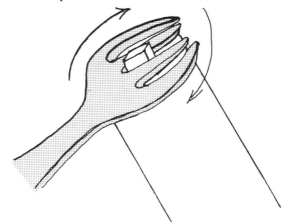

You will feel the spring become tighter and harder to turn. (Take care not to overwind it or you can break the spring.) As spring tension increases, I sometimes grasp the roller between my knees to keep it from unwinding itself again. Now tilt the roller so the teeth catch in the spear notch and lock the spring in place.

A TOO TIGHT SPRING can be adjusted by rolling the shade up to the top , taking it down and unrolling it about six inches. Replace on brackets and roll it up again. Repeat until the tension is right.

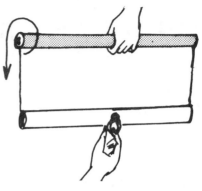

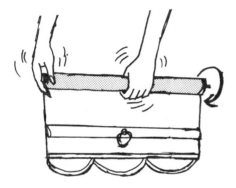

A TOO LOOSE SPRING or a shade that will not roll up easily--first check the installation. If the bracket is not rubbing or bent or loose, pull the shade down about 12 inches and remove from brackets. Carefully roll about 6 inches of shade onto the roller, then replace. Repeat until the operation is smooth.

BRACKET PROBLEMS may be indicated if the shade does not stay put easily, or if it falls out of the brackets. Are the brackets straight and level? Is there 1/16" to 1/8" leeway for smooth action? Does the fabric rub against the bracket? Are brackets too far apart? The pin may be pulled out slightly to lengthen a roller that is not more than 1/4" short.

If shade is rolling with difficulty, be sure pin has been put into the roller straight.

Never drive a nail or staple longer than 1/4" into the mechanism end. Do not oil or take metal caps off the mechanism.

When installing brackets, it is best to use screws (or plaster bolts) if possible. Nails can work loose and affect the fit of the shade.

46

SPEARLINING

When you wish shades on side by side windows to stop at the same level automatically when raised, use a technique called Spearlining before you attach shades to rollers.

Lay two (or more) bare rollers down on a piece of paper. (The paper is to protect the surface so you can draw lines with felt pen or pencil.) Position the rollers so the teeth which engage the notch on the end mechanism are at exactly the same location. Hold the rollers firmly and draw a line on the first roller. Set it aside and draw a line on the second roller, etc. The guide lines you have just drawn are now "synchronized". Attach shades to rollers along the guide lines, place in brackets at windows. The shades will now stop evenly side by side.

With a permanent marker place a mark or dot on the wheel and the teeth of the roller. Then if the spring gets bumped or moved, you can re-align the shade easily.

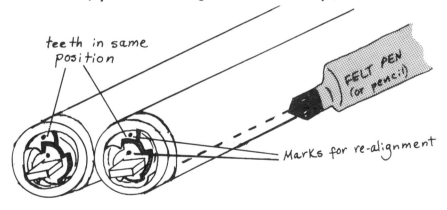

teeth in same position

FELT PEN (or pencil)

Marks for re-alignment

SHORTENING TIP

If you plan to use the same shade on a roller you are shortening, roll the shade up evenly and push a tack in it at the width your new shade should be. Note: This is the SHADE width; the roller will be longer. Remove the tack

and unroll the shade. The holes left by the tack will mark
your cutting line. Before removing the shade from the roller, draw a guide line on the roller along the top edge of
the shade. Take the shade off the roller, cut to fit. Replace along line you drew. Use tape or staples to secure
the shade to the roller.

SHADE TRIM IDEAS

wide variety of moods and special effects can be created through the use of trims and design on shades. Here are some ideas for roller shades.

- Use a strip of cotton or linen fused across the shade. Add narrow trim down the middle or on each side.

- Stencil a design that you create, or draw a design to coordinate with other fabrics in the room. This is particularly effective on a plastic or solid color custom shade.

- Applique motifs from fabric--single flowers or objects, or strips of border trim. Glue or fuse in place. They may be stitched on if you are careful not to stretch the fabric.

- Decorative pulls can be crocheted or macramed. They may be metal or wood objects. Wood curtain rings make interesting pulls, too.

- Wallpaper motifs may be added to purchased shades. Glue design motif in the hem/border area. Do not roll up the decorated portion.

- Gimp, fringe, braid, etc. can be glued or fused to a shade border.

SHADE TRIM DESIGN IDEAS

Following are a wide variety of shade trim design ideas. The directions for making the pattern for the borders are on page in the section on Finishing Touches.

Remember that these shade trim ideas can also be used for cornices and valances. NOTE: A complete section on cornices and valances can be found in Decorating With Fabric/An Idea Book by Judy Lindahl.

Special effects can be achieved on the shades by using two or more rows of trim. (Designs are usually sketched with one row indicated). Tassels may be added or removed for differing effects on many designs.

To continue a design for a wider shade, contemplate two possibilities:
1) Stretch out the design, enlarging it proportionately.
2) Repeat more of the design--extending the sides. For very wide shades, this is the best method.

NOTE: Be sure to make a paper pattern to test design first. See p. 42.
Following are two examples of enlarged designs:

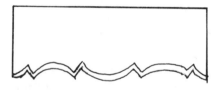

Basic Design #1

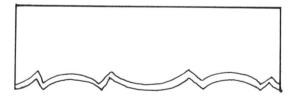

Enlarged by proportion

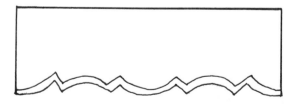

Same size--sides extended

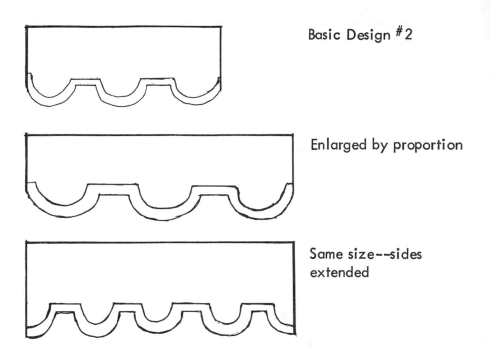

Basic Design #2

Enlarged by proportion

Same size--sides extended

SHADE HEM/CORNICE/VALANCE DECORATIVE EDGES

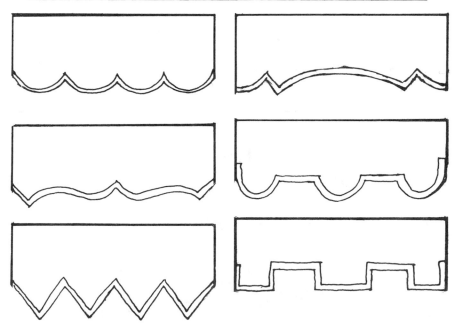

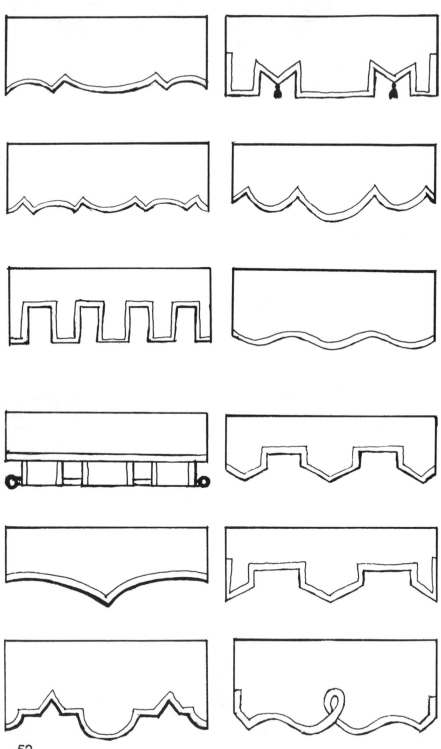

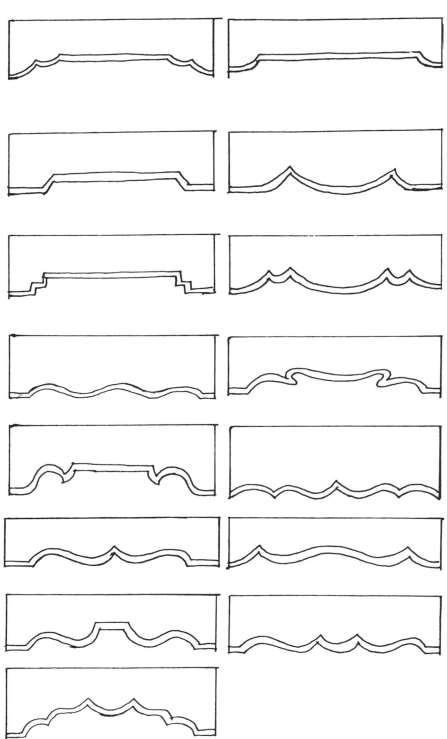

53

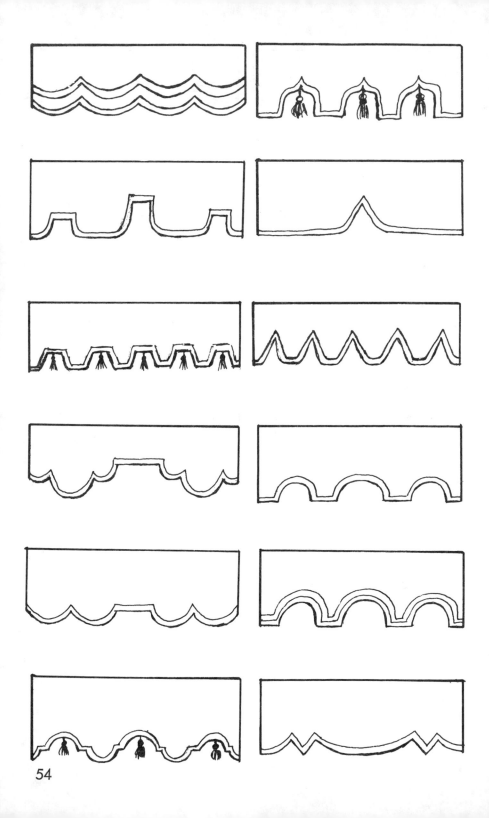

54

LOOP TRIM IDEAS

SELF LOOP

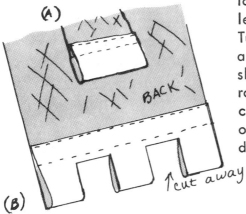

To determine length: Add 18" to window opening length. Laminate the shade. Turn shade back on itself (A), and stitch two lines to form slat channel. Then cut out rod straps (B). Glue trim across front, just above cutouts, if desired. Slip rod or dowel through loops.

STITCHED SELF FABRIC LOOPS

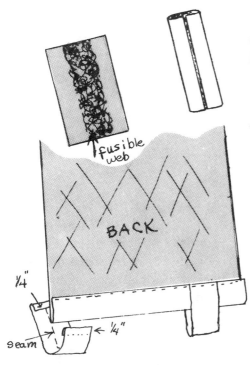

Press 1 1/4" to back side of shade. Stitch. Make pieces for straps twice the finished width and twice the finished length + 1/2". Lay a strip of fusible web which is cut the size of the finished strap, down the center. Bring raw edges together and fuse, making a strap. Turn top and bottom edges under 1/4". Fuse strap to shade to secure and keep from shifting, then stitch in place to slat seams as shown.

Strap width and number of straps depends on width and proportion of shade.

LOOPS FROM PURCHASED TRIM

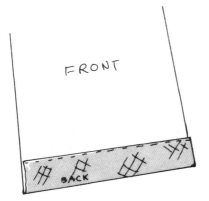

Turn slat hem to front side of shade. Stitch or fuse. (Fusing can be done on all fabric methods--except commercial backings).

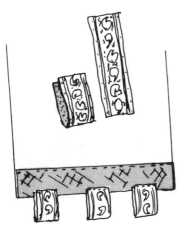

Cut number of trim loops desired. Allow twice the length of loop needed, plus 2".
Stitch loops to bottom front edge of shade.

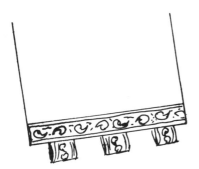

Cut strip of trim width of shade plus 1/2". Turn ends under 1/4" and fuse. Fuse or glue trim in place on top of slat pocket and even with bottom edge.

POSITIONING LOOPS AND RODS

There are a few details to consider on loop hem treatments. The length and location of the rod is dependent to a degree on the type of bracket and mounting used with your shade.

For Inside Mount

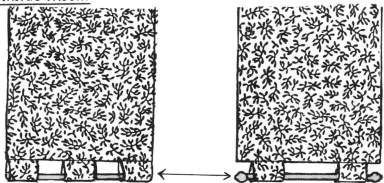

rod must fit
inside window frame

For Outside Mount

rod ends may extend beyond shade

DIRECTORY OF SHADE BRACKETS

STANDARD INSIDE BRACKET
The most common type, it may
be used wherever there is
enough depth inside a window
frame to accommodate the roller. This type bracket may be
reversed, that is, you may
place the spear bracket on the
right frame and the round pin
bracket on the left. You may
also purchase a special reverse bracket.

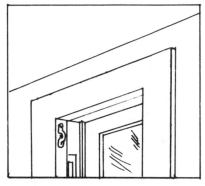

Conventional Roll

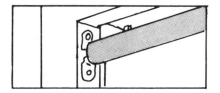

Reverse Roll

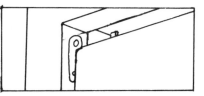

INSIDE EXTENSION BRACKET (Footless Bracket)
Mounted inside window frame.
Requires less space than inside
bracket. Extends slightly into
room away from window. Often
used for narrow framed windows, or to extend the shade
outward to clear casement
cranks, door hinges, etc.

RANCH BRACKET
Clear plastic version of the inside extension bracket. Curved
to follow contour of narrow, contemporary window frames.

SASH RUN (Boston) BRACKET
Special bracket for use with all-wood, double-hung windows. Mounted at the top of the sash run (track where the window slides up and down.) Has a 'bumper' to stop the window when it is raised. The shade is mounted reverse roll to clear the window below. This results in a shade close to the glass, overlapping the frame, for an almost light-proof installation.

OUTSIDE BRACKET
Mounted on trim or wall adjacent to window. Used when window is not deep enough to accommodate an inside bracket. Used for shades wider than the window, to eliminate light streaks at sides, or just to give the illusion of a wider window. If brackets are mounted on wall, an expansion bolt or anchor is recommended.

COMBINATION BRACKET
These are dual purpose brackets that hold both a window shade and a curtain rod, and are available in fixed or adjustable types. They eliminate the need for two sets of brackets, making a cleaner line at the window.

CEILING BRACKETS

Very useful on ceiling-high windows, bow windows or those with deep recesses. They may be installed on the ceiling itself. They give standard windows an illusion of extra height. Reverse roll is recommended unless a cornice or valance covers the roller. Useful on an overhang above a window or on double-hung aluminum windows.

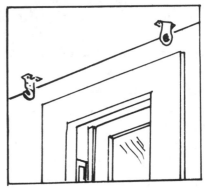

DOUBLE BRACKETS

Designed for two shades at the same window, usually one is translucent, the other a room-darkener. The roomside shade gets reverse roll in many cases to avoid interference with the other. Available in outside and inside mount, or for inside installations two single brackets may be mounted one above the other.

Similar brackets can be installed at center of the window, so that one, a bottom-up shade, covers the upper sash, a regular shade pulls down to cover lower sash, permitting both windows to be opened without causing the shades to flap. Many institutions, particularly schools, use them.

HORIZONTAL INSTALLATION

For skylights inside or ceiling brackets may be used, depending on whether the installation is within the frame or on the face of the skylight. For very large skylights stretched wires are used to keep the shade taut. The shade is operated by a cord and pulley system similar to those in bottoms-up shades.

60

BOTTOMS-UP SHADES

If a shade is mounted at the bottom of a window, it pulls up by means of a pulley mechanism. This is especially effective when privacy is desired, and for cathedral type windows which require slanting shade top to fit the window contour. Brackets for sill mounting or outside brackets are particularly adapted to bottoms-up use. Special brackets may also be ordered.

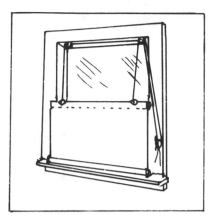

There are a variety of ways in which the pulley mechanism can be attached or concealed or eliminated.

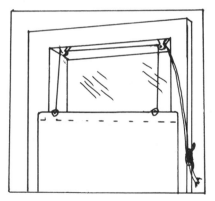

Top Mount Pulley

Sketch shows top mount pulley with cords tied off on awning cleat, but it is also possible to use a lock pulley, which catches and holds the cords in place like a venetian blind lock. (see below)

Slat Pulley

In this version the cords run through the inside of a special hollow slat. This conceals most of the cord. A lock pulley is used at the top to anchor the cord at various levels.

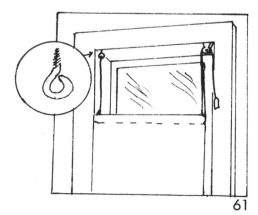

The following are two ideas for avoiding pulleys and cords on the bottoms-up shade.

Use inside bracket for oval curtain rod. Mount brackets at positions on window frame most likely to be preferred when shade is pulled up. Pull shade up and set slat or rod in the brackets. Slat must be longer than shade to fit in brackets.

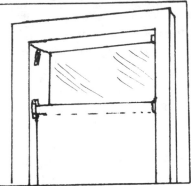

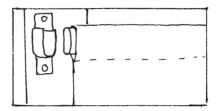

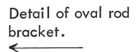

Detail of oval rod bracket.

Use a spring tension curtain rod in hem of bottoms-up shade. Good especially if shade is not moved a lot; but rubber tips of rod can cause some worn spots on frame in time.

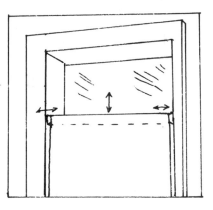

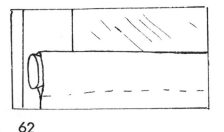

Detail of tension curtain rod.

WINDOW TYPES

There is a shade for every window and a window for every shade. The following discussion of window types should help you make some choices.

DOUBLE-HUNG WINDOW

Two sashes move up and down. Most have a wood sash, and sash-run brackets are usually the choice. If you wish to light-proof the window, select outside brackets. Windows with aluminum sash usually do not have enough room for an inside bracket, so an extension or outside bracket is often chosen.

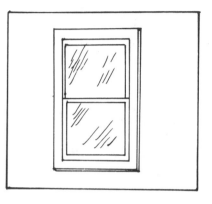

PICTURE WINDOWS

On combination types with fixed center sash and double-hung, casement, or awning windows at the sides, the whole window may be treated as one; with one large shade hung from the outside or ceiling brackets. Or treat it as three separate windows. If divider frames are not flush with adjacent wall, a combination of outside and footless brackets may be used to equalize the two. The outside brackets would be mounted on the divider frame, the footless brackets on jambs at either side of the window. Use

reverse roll if cranks or handles are present. For multi panel type windows one big shade is preferable, hung on outside or ceiling brackets, or inside brackets if there is enough room.

SLIDING WINDOWS

Usually one pane is fixed and one is movable. If set directly in plaster, use either outside or ceiling brackets. However, sliding windows set in wood sometimes give enough space for an inside or footless bracket.

SLIDING GLASS DOORS

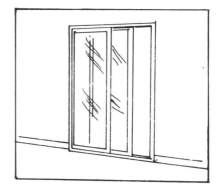

These are most often of aluminum, occasionally of wood. Both types are handled alike. Shades may be hung from the ceiling or from outside brackets on the adjacent wall. In the latter, use reverse roll so shade clears door handle. Use one large shade or separate ones corresponding to each door.

BAY WINDOW

Use separate shades for each window. Select the bracket needed according to the type of window frame and style.

CASEMENT WINDOWS

They open like a door; sometimes only part of the window
is movable. Most important
is to mount the shade so it
does not interfere with locks
or handle cranks. Use a
footless bracket, or reverse
roll on an inside bracket to
provide the extra clearance.
Use outside brackets for metal casements not deep enough
for inside brackets.

BOW WINDOW

If bow is slight, one large
shade may be hung straight
across window area with ceiling brackets. Otherwise, treat
as a bay window with separate
shades for each section hung
from ceiling brackets.

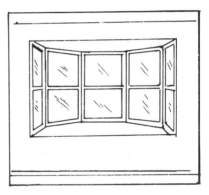

DOOR WINDOWS

French doors and half-length
windows as on kitchen doors
are treated alike. Shades are
mounted on the door frame
with outside brackets, conventional roll. Be sure shade is
not so wide that it interferes
with the door knob.

SKYLIGHT, STUDIO, AND DOME WINDOWS

These types of windows may be fitted with special installations mounted horizontally or on the slant. They are drawn with a pulley and cord mechanism.

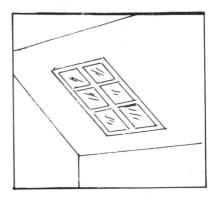

CATHEDRAL WINDOWS

Slanted top windows like this are easily handled with the bottoms-up technique. Shades are installed at the base of the window, drawing up from the sill on a pulley. The shade top is cut to conform to the slant of the window. If the slanted windows are above regular windows, you may use the same shade cloth below in a pull-down shade for overall unity.

DORMER WINDOWS

These are usually deeply recessed and are best treated with inside brackets or with ceiling brackets.

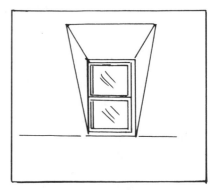

CORNER WINDOWS
One technique is to use ceiling brackets. Another is with outside brackets on wall area just above windows. If the frame between windows is very narrow, there is the possibility of shade rollers interfering with each other. In this case, one shade can be hung slightly above the other and a cornice installed to conceal the irregularity. If there is no room on the inside of the window frames, shades may be hung from inside or footless brackets.

AWNING WINDOWS
These windows open to the outside and are operated by a crank or handle.
Top: Jalousie - Use outside bracket on trim, allowing clearance for the crank.
Center: Bank of awning sash - Use inside or footless bracket with reverse roll to allow for the crank.
Lower: Fixed sash on top, awning sash below - Use inside or footless bracket with reverse roll to clear any projection. Bottoms-up is not practical with these types because of the crank, nor with the combination fixed sash and awning window since ventilation is at the bottom.

67

ROMAN SHADES

Adozen different kinds of Roman Shades? Impossible!! Not so--you'll find as you read through the pages that follow. This exciting window treatment actually encompasses a whole family of variations. It would be possible to have Roman-type shades in nearly every room in the house--and have each room different. Fantastic!

Each of the variations builds on the Basic Flat Roman Shade. Once you thoroughly understand this basic shade, you can reach out to create interesting and exciting changes in the texture and dimension of your shades.

JUST WHAT IS A ROMAN SHADE?

The basic shade is flat when down, but pleats up when cords are pulled to raise it. These cords are usually strung through eyelets, rings or grommets. and then through screw eyes or pulleys on a 1" x 2" mounting board. Cords wind off on an awning cleat placed at the side of the window.

Lowered Position   Raised Position

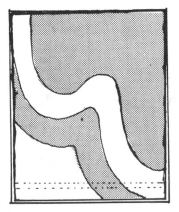
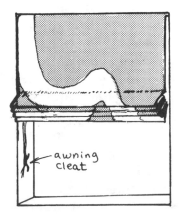

awning cleat

The rings are placed in even parallel rows beginning at the
top of a weight rod. This rod gives stability and even hang
to the shade. It is also important that the shade be constructed and mounted square, or the even hang will be affected.

Unlike a roller shade, the excess fabric does not disappear
when the shade is raised. It stacks up in pleats or folds.

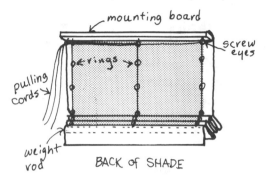

BACK of SHADE

In this book shade directions are arranged so that flat shade
methods are discussed first. Then come those which add
length, thus allowing for tucks and pleats which create surface texture and sharp pleating action. Next the addition of
width creates controlled softness as in cloud and balloon
shades. And finally the addition of length and width creates
the elegant Austrian shade.

FABRICS

The type of fabric used will have an affect on the look of the
finished shade. For the crisp look of the flat Roman or Accordian, sturdy firm fabrics work best. If you want to use
lighter weight or lace fabric, it may be necessary to line it
or stiffen it to add more body. Even then, the look will not
be exactly the same as would be achieved by heavier fabric.

Cloud, balloon, and Austrian shades will be at their best in
softer fabrics that drape easily. But here, too, the rules can
be broken. I have seen balloon shades of moire and heavy
hopsacking. However, they require more care and lots of
hand dressing to achieve the desired look.

Fabric may need to be seamed to create the needed width at the window. If so, seam one full width center panel with two or more equal strips at the sides, matching design where needed. Try to plan for a row of rings to fall behind a seam.

Part Width	Full Width	Part Width

Most professionals feel shades hang better and look better from the outside if they are lined. However, Roman shades made of heavier fabrics or open-work casements may be left unlined. Cloud, balloon, and Austrian shades are almost always unlined so they will drape more softly and easily.

MOUNTING

How you plan to mount your shade influences all your measurements, so that decision must be made early.

A 1" x 2" board is usually used for mounting the shade. This board may be painted white or covered with extra lining fabric if desired. If a cornice or valance is to be added, the board may be 1" x 3" or 1" x 4" to allow clearance for the shade.

Note: A complete section of cornice and valance ideas can be found in Decorating With Fabric/An Idea Book. Ordering information is on the last page of this book.

Inside and outside mounts are the types most frequently used.

INSIDE MOUNT

The shade fits entirely within an opening. Accuracy in constructing and mounting the shade is more critical because the opening defines and outlines the shade. A popular mount because the shade sits back so the operating mechanism is completely concealed.

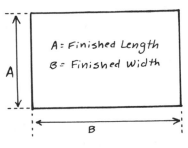

A = Finished Length
B = Finished Width

70

Cut a 1" x 2" board to fit inside the opening. Fasten by screwing through the board into the window frame or by fastening angle irons to the underside of the board and to the side of the window frame.

OUTSIDE MOUNT

The shade may be installed above the opening—on the wall or ceiling. This allows the stacked pleats to clear the opening to give more light or clearance.

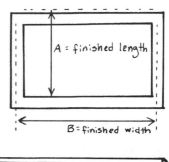

Use angle irons to mount the board above the window on window frame or wall, as preferred.

ADDITIONAL MOUNTING IDEAS

TENSION ROD

For smaller windows a 1-1/2" casing may be sewn at the top of the shade. The spring tension rod is slipped through this casing and fitted in place at the window. Screw eyes are mounted directly into the window frame above each row or rings. The shade is strung in the regular manner with the strain being taken by the screw eyes. The limitations are on the size and weight of shade that the tension rod can support.

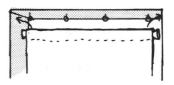

BOTTOM UP

For a bottom up mounting the 1"x2" board is secured to the window sill or floor. (Mount the board toward the back of the sill as the pleats will stack and lie forward.) Two cords are anchored at the weight bar and will be the pulling cords. Two cords are anchored to screw eyes at the top and bottom of the window. (They are tied only after being threaded through the rings.) These are the tracking cords that hold the shade in place as it is pulled. Since no cords are usually placed in the middle of the shade, best choices will be methods with dowels or tucks stitched across the pleats to help retain the sharpness and shape. At the very least, the edges of the pleats may need to be pressed crisply.

This shade can be used on a window placed high on the wall. Starting the shade at the floor gives the look of a full length window.

HINT: A cornice or valance conceals cords and screw eyes.

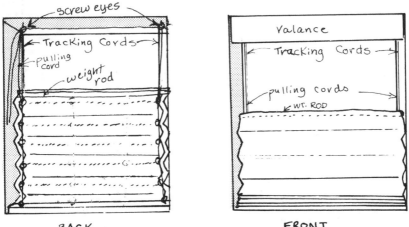

BACK   FRONT

TOP DOWN/BOTTOM UP - THE ATHEY SHADE

Two shades are mounted and rigged in the window so one raises from the bottom up as described above, and the other raises in the conventional manner.

This is particularly effective on long windows or where the appearance of a floor to ceiling window is desired.

The screw eyes for the bottom up shade are mounted slightly behind the screw eyes for the conventional shade. String one set of cords to the left side of the window frame and one set to the right side.

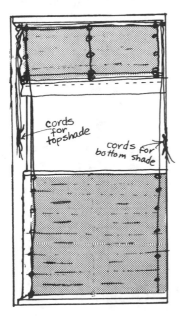

cords for topshade

cords for bottom shade

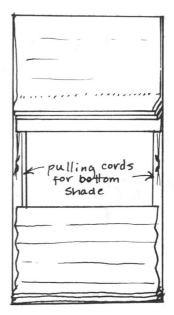

pulling cords for bottom shade

ROLLER MOUNT

For this mounting method the shade is mounted in the standard manner to the 1" x 2" or 1" x 3" mounting board, but the cords are secured to a wood roller mounted with ceiling brackets to the underside of the mounting board.

Note: 1/4" satin or grossgrain ribbon may be substituted for the cords.

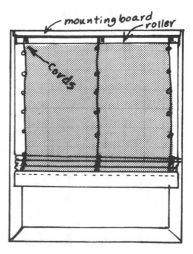

mounting board

roller

Cords

At least one extra pleat length must be included to allow the tug required to initiate the roller action.

To adapt this method for accordian shades, the cords or ribbons are run through the holes in the shade, then they are brought to the back side where they are secured to the roller.

Side View - Conventional   Side View - Accordian
Roman Shade   Shade

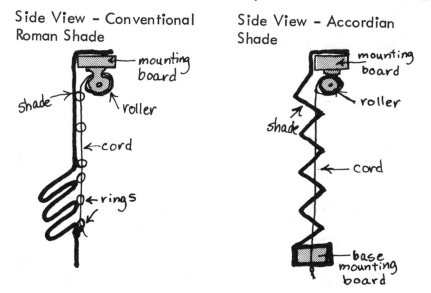

HEM DEPTH & RING PLACEMENT

Another decision that affects finished measurements of the shade is hem depth. The standard hem depth on a Roman shade is one half the distance between rows of rings.

For example if rings are 6" apart the hem would be 3" deep. Thus when the cords are pulled raising the shade, the hem is covered by the folds of the shade.

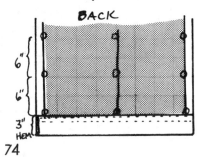

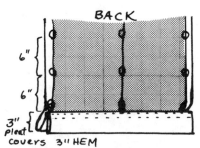

The illustrations in this book are based on this formula--
rings 6" apart, 3" hem.

If you desire a band of hem to show when the shade is
raised, the hem must be made deeper and the first row of
rings and the weight rod are placed higher on the shade.

For example if a 3" decorative hem is to remain exposed
when the cords are pulled and the shade is raised, a 6" hem
must be constructed.

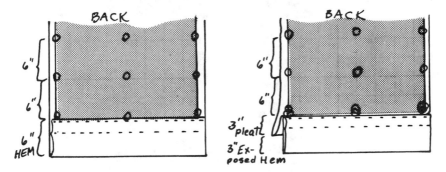

While it is possible to stitch on a separate hem to create
added length in the hem area, it is wise to consider the
hem type you prefer when making original calculations.

Note: If you do not plan to add a cornice or valance, you
may wish to add a row or rings just below or near the mounting board. This holds the shade in and keeps it from 'pok-
ing out' at the top and revealing the mounting board when
the shade is raised. You may wish to sew the rings on, then
decide whether or not you need them when you string the
completed shade.

BASIC ROMAN SHADES

These shades are flat when down, often resembling a roller shade. They take a minimum of fabric and show a print or design to best advantage since there are no pleats or tucks to interfere.

Standard Method

I have found this to be my favorite basic method. It is fast and accurate because the face fabric is prepared on the work surface first, then the lining is positioned right on the face fabric. Thus a minimum of handling and pressing is required. Even though the faced hem technique takes a bit more time, it is an attractive finish since only lining fabric shows on the outside of the house. (Side hems are almost always concealed by the window casings.)

Measuring

Width = Finished width plus 3"
        (Remember to add for seam allowances if fabric must
         be pieced to achieve necessary width)
Length = Finished length plus 3"

Lining = Finished width (Add for seam allowances if lining must be pieced for necessary width)
Facing Strip = 5" deep x finished width plus 2"

1. Cut, seam, and press shade
   fabric--keeping it square.
   If fabric tends to ravel easily
   zig-zag side edges, turn under 1/4" or treat with glue
   (see p. 40).

   Lay right side down on cutting
   board or work surface. Square
   fabric if needed. Measure and
   mark finished width. Turn excess at sides and press in equal
   hems. (Approx. 1-1/2" each.)

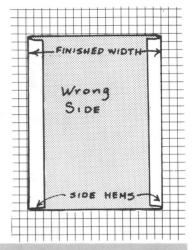

Note: The fabric was cut 3" wider to allow for 1-1/2"
side hems. This may change slightly due to zig-zagging,
turn of cloth, steam shrinkage or handling of fabric.

2. Lay lining fabric on top of
   shade fabric and press smoothly in place. Mark it using the
   shade fabric as guide. Cut it
   to fit. Slip the lining under
   the side hems. Smooth and
   press the two together. Pin
   the shade and lining together
   in a few places.

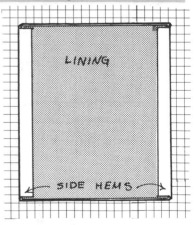

3. Slip facing strip under shade.
   Center and pin even with bottom edge, leaving 1" exten-
   ding at each side. Stitch a
   1/2" seam allowance along
   bottom edge.

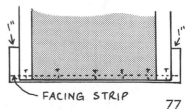

FACING STRIP

77

Press facing strip to wrong side of the shade.

Fold and press side extensions in so they do not show from right side. Insert a strip of fusible web between the facing layers. Fuse. See p. 11.

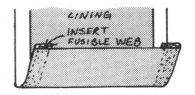

4. Turn and press top edge of facing strip down to make a 3" hem. Stitch along top edge, then again 1" down to form the rod pocket.

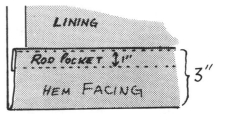

5. Realign shade on cutting board or work surface, lining side up. Mark placement of rings - keeping rows even and parallel. The first row is placed at the top of the weight bar and 1" in from side edges so side hems are held in place by rings.

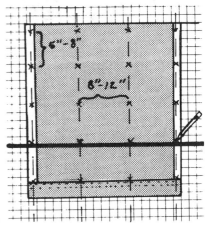

To speed marking and keep it accurate use a long ruler or aluminum bar to lay across the shade. Draw very lightly with pencil. After all lines are completed in one direction, lay ruler in the opposite direction and make a small mark at the intersection of each line.

Vertical rows are usually 8" to 12" apart, horizontal rows are 5" to 8" with 6" being the general spacing.

6. Rings can be sewn by hand, but it will be faster to use the zig-zag button stitch on the sewing machine. After a ring is secured with about 8-10 stitches, lock the stitches by allowing the needle to penetrate the same spot for a few stitches. Then move on to the next ring without cutting

the threads. Sew as many rings as practical before you stop. Clip threads with a gentle touch so you don't pull out any stitches.

Reinforce bottom row of rings since they are the ones that carry the weight of the shade.

Note: For some fabrics it will help to insert a corsage pin through the fabric under the ring. Stitch over both pin and ring to create a space or shank, then remove the pin. This eliminates a pull or pucker on the front caused by tight stitches.

Hint: When sewing by hand you may wish to change thread color for the different colors in the fabric. When I do this I thread several needles--each with the appropriate color. Then as I need to change color, I have the needle all ready to go. OR you may use a clear nylon thread for hand or machine sewing. Be sure it is resistant to sunlight (Coats and Clark Crystal) and watch the pressing temperature, as some threads are very heat sensitive.

7. Insert a 3/8" solid metal rod weight bar in rod pocket. Rods are available in hardware, drapery shops, home improvement centers, and businesses specializing in Iron Works (see yellow pages.) Cut rod 1/2" narrower than finished length.

Position screw eyes in mounting board ex-actly above each row of rings. You may need one extra eye to help distribute the strain of the pulling cords. See illustration.

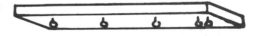

Hint: If the shade is very wide, small pulleys or roller brackets (available through drapery supply) can be used in place of screw eyes. They save wear and tear on cords.

Staple or tack the shade in place on the top of the mounting board.

staple   mounting board

FRONT

8. String the shade. Cut lengths of non-stretchy cord, one for each row of rings. Each will be a different length, but must go up shade and across top of window with excess at side for pulling.

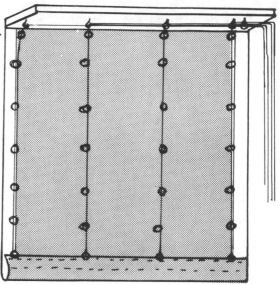

9. Tie cords securely to bottom ring, thread through rings and screw eyes. Final adjusting of cords will be done when shade is in window. Tighten so tension is equal on each cord.

NOTE: Screw eyes at end where all cords come through must be large enough so cords don't bind up.

10. Mount shade in window. Adjust cord tension. Mount an awning cleat (see hardware) at the side of the window to wind off the cords when shade is pulled.

Traditional Method

In this method lining and shade fabric are sewn together first. It requires more handling of the shade, and demands accurate cutting and stitching to maintain the dimensions of the shade.

Measuring
Width = Finished width plus 3" for side hems
　　　　(Add for seam allowances if fabric must be pieced.)
Length = Finished length plus 5-1/2"
Lining = Same length as shade fabric, finished width minus 1"

1. Lay lining on shade fabric right sides together. (Shade fabric will be larger.)

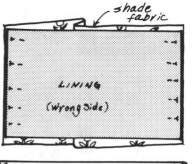

2. Stitch 1/2" side seams. Pull inside out like a pillow case, and press so that lining is centered. Turn up 3-1/2" hem. Press.

3. Turn raw edge under 1/2" Stitch hem. Stitch again 1" down to form pocket for weight bar.

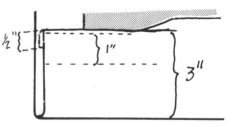

OR For shaped hem turn fabric back on itself, right sides together. Stitch hem shape, clip, turn and press. (You may need to add extra length to shade for a deeply shaped hem.)

Trim may be sewn or glued to hem if desired.

4. Follow steps 5 through 10 on Standard Method.

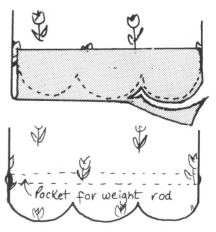

Ring Tape Method

Roman shade ring tape is a special notion with pre-spaced rings sewn to a twill tape, which can then be sewn to a shade. It is usually considered to be a time-saver, not a money saver. For example one yard of tape yields eight rings at an average cost of $1.00 per yard. The same eight rings purchased separately would cost about $.20.

If I do use ring tape, rather than stitching along each edge as the manufacturer recommends, I prefer to zig-zag over each ring, catching it through shade and lining. This makes thread less noticeable on the front and reduces chances of pulling and puckering of the shade fabric.

Be sure you PRESHRINK the cotton twill tape if you plan to wash your shade. Even if you plan to clean it, preshrinking is a good idea.

1. Follow steps 1 through 4 on Standard Method.

2. Cut Roman shade tapes so the first row of rings starts at the top of the weight bar.

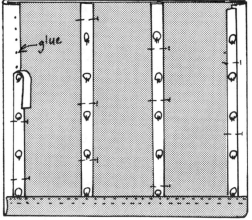

3. Lightly mark vertical position of the tapes. Run a thin line or row of dots of fabric glue (Wilhold, Quik) along the lines just marked. Align rings and press the tapes in place. Secure with a few pins. (Be sure rings on side tapes lie on top of side hems so stitching will catch hems.)

4. Follow steps 6 through 10 on Standard Method.

Ringless Tape Method

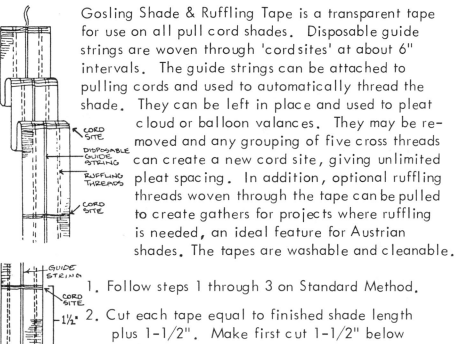

Gosling Shade & Ruffling Tape is a transparent tape for use on all pull cord shades. Disposable guide strings are woven through 'cord sites' at about 6" intervals. The guide strings can be attached to pulling cords and used to automatically thread the shade. They can be left in place and used to pleat cloud or balloon valances. They may be removed and any grouping of five cross threads can create a new cord site, giving unlimited pleat spacing. In addition, optional ruffling threads woven through the tape can be pulled to create gathers for projects where ruffling is needed, an ideal feature for Austrian shades. The tapes are washable and cleanable.

1. Follow steps 1 through 3 on Standard Method.

2. Cut each tape equal to finished shade length plus 1-1/2". Make first cut 1-1/2" below cord site.

3. Slip tapes under hem 1-1/2" with cord site just above hem edge. Place a pin at each cord site. (Position tapes about 3/4" from side edges, so tapes cover cut edge. Equally space other tapes.

4. Stitch along top edge of hem, but do NOT catch guide strings. Stitch again 1" down to form the rod pocket.

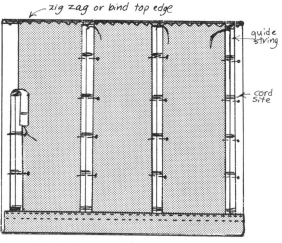

zig zag or bind top edge

5. Zig zag top edge of shade or bind with bias tape. Do NOT catch guide strings.

6. Tack tapes securely beside or just below cord sites--by hand or with zig zag stitches OR stitch down the edges of the tapes (best on laces or prints where stitches will not show).

7. Wrap mounting board with lining fabric (glue, fuse, or tack fabric in place. Center shade on board and staple or tack in place.

8. Thread Gosling Cord through cord sites by one of the following methods: A) Tie disposable guide string and pulling cord securely together. Pull gently on disposable string, and the cord will thread through the cord sites automatically OR B) Remove disposable guide strings from tapes. Thread cord through cord sites using large tapestry needle. Catch groups of five cords at desired intervals. Be sure all cord sites are level across the shade.

DISPOSABLE CORD

PULLING CORD

9. Thread pull cord on large-eye needle and stitch to top of bottom hem with reinforcing stitches. A dab of glue keeps it secure. Each cord must be anchored securely to the hem since the weight of the shade is centered here.

10. Insert 3/8" brass, iron rod (treated to prevent rust), OR galvanized metal rod into rod pocket. Rods are available from hardware, drapery shops, home improvement centers, etc.

ROD POCKET

HEM

11. Mount shade at window. Add awning cleat for securing the pulling cords.

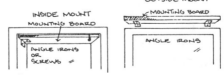

OUTSIDE MOUNT

INSIDE MOUNT
MOUNTING BOARD

MOUNTING BOARD

ANGLE IRONS
OR
SCREWS

ANGLE IRONS

PLEATED & TUCKED VARIATIONS

All of the methods within this group are made basically the same as a standard Roman shade. The only variable is that each shade adds tucks or pleats which form surface texture and sharp pleating action. To allow for the pleats and tucks additional length must be incorporated into each shade.

Dowel Tucks & Screw Eyes

This method creates a very smooth hanging shade because the dowel (or slat) in each tuck lends weight and support to the shade and keeps the fabric taut. A metal weight bar is not needed, since each tuck is individually weighted. Fabrics unsuited to this technique include some sheers, and prints whose design impact could be interrupted by the tucks.

MEASURING

To determine the length of fabric calculate the number of horizontal rows or rings on the body of the shade. Add 1-1/2" of length for each row. (The illustration shows 5 rows, hence 7-1/2" of extra length.)

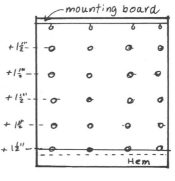

1. Follow steps 1 through 4 on standard method. Place shade right side down on cutting board or work surface.

2. Draw faint line on back side of shade 3/4" above top of hem. Then draw a line every 7-1/2" on the body of the shade.

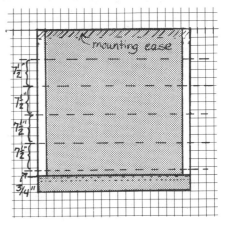

3. Fold and pin the shade on each line. Stitch a 3/4" tuck across the shade. The tucks all lie on the back of the shade.

4. Slip 3/8" dowels through the tucks. Poke a hole on top of the dowels 1" from each side edge. Use an awl or sharp nail. Insert a small screw eye in each hole.

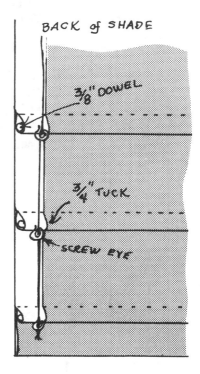

BACK of SHADE

   On wide shades one or two more screw eyes may be needed across the shade for support. On narrower shades they are needed only at the side.

5. Tie a large knot in the end of each cord so it will not slip through the screw eye.

6. Follow steps 8 through 10 for standard shade.

FRONT DOWEL TUCKS

Make the shade according to directions above EXCEPT sew the tucks and insert dowels on the FRONT of the shade. Sew rings behind the tucks. Make the dowels just short enough that you can close the ends of the tucks with hand stitches.

POLE SHADE

For this style 1" to 1-1/4" dia-meter dowels are inserted at in-tervals in stitched casings. The space between poles is 10" to 12". Rings are sewn behind each pole or screw eyes can be used.

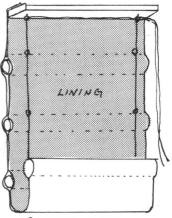

BACK OF SHADE

Measuring

Fabric and lining are cut the finished width plus 1"; the finished length plus 1" per pole plus seam allowance and mount-ing ease.

Place right sides of fabrics together and mark positions for casings. Stitch as indicated by arrows, then turn right side out and press. Mark and stitch casings for poles. Sew on rings, insert poles, mount and string. You will probably want to paint the ends of the poles, or glue a circle of matching fabric to them.

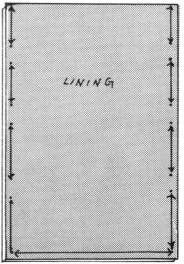

Note: You may wish to use fusible web under seam allow-ances to keep poles from catch-ing on the casings as they are inserted.

Front Tucks with Slats

This method pro-
duces a very tailor-
ed shade with tex-
tural interest crea-
ted by the front
tucks. Due to the
slats the pleating
action is sharp and
smooth and the fab-
ric stays taut. Front
pleats create a hori-
zontal shadow when
the light is behind
a lowered shade.

This method is very
effective with heav-
ier fabrics that do
not require lining,
especially many upholstery fabrics.

MEASURING

To determine length calculate
the number of horizontal rows
of rings on the body of the
shade and add 2" for the bottom row and 3" for all others.
(This shade will have a 1-1/2"
self hem. Rows will be spaced
9" apart on finished shade.)

mounting board

+3"
+3"
+3"
+3"
+2

1. Follow steps 1 and 2 for Standard Method.

2. Turn down 1/2" then 1-1/2"
   along the bottom edge to
   form a 1-1/2" hem. Stitch.

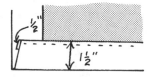

3. Align and square shade right side down on cutting board or work surface. Measure up 12" from bottom edge and fold shade back on itself. Pin and mark a 1-1/2" tuck.

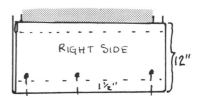

RIGHT SIDE

12"

1½"

4. Continue to fold shade back at 12" intervals. Pin, mark, and stitch remaining tucks.

5. Sew rings 1" from each side edge behind the tucks and at top of bottom hem. On wide shades an additional row or two of rings may be needed for support. On narrow shades rings are needed only at side hems.

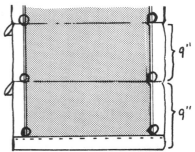

9"

9"

6. Insert wood slats (roller shade slats from shade shop, or thin wood strips). Follow steps 8 through 10, Standard Method.

Front & Back Tucks with Eyelets

This method gives a tailored shade that pleats very neatly and sharply. Optional 1/8" dowels in the front tucks add dimension and keep the shade smooth. A darker line is produced by the shadow of the front tuck when light is behind the shade. This is one of my favorite methods not only for the look, but because no rings are involved. Eyelets

are inserted through the back tucks with an eyelet plier, and pulling cords are strung through the eyelets.

MEASURING

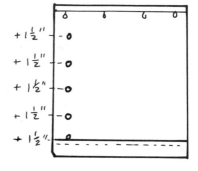

To determine length add 1-1/2" for each horizontal row of rings.

1. Follow steps 1 through 4 of Standard Method.

2. Draw a faint line 3/8" above top of hem facing. This is the fold line for the first back tuck. Align shade on cutting board graph or work surface. Now draw a faint line every 7-1/2" on the remainder of the shade. (Short marks 3/8" on either side of the 7-1/2" lines are optional, but helpful for accuracy in stitching.) Fold and stitch all back tucks.

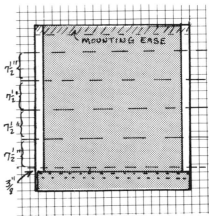

3. Fold shade back on itself, wrong sides together, so two back tucks are even. Pin. Continue with the rest of the shade, then stitch 3/8" front tucks.

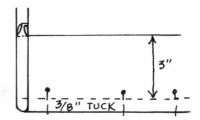

4. Mark eyelet positions on back tucks--1" from side edges and across body of shade.

5. Using eyelet plier punch holes in fabric, then insert 1/8" eyelets.

6. Insert 1/8" dowels in front pleats.

7. Tie a knot in ends of pulling cords so they will not go through eyelets, then string and mount as for Standard Method steps 8 through 10.

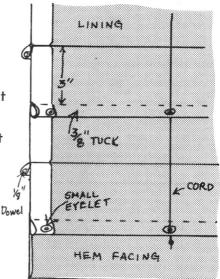

Loose Tucks with Eyelets

This is a great favorite of custom workrooms. One reason may be that it can be made entirely without sewing if you use a fabric glue on the hem or catch it in the eyelets. Most home sewers will not have access to heavy duty grommet setters available through window products or tent and awning suppliers, but a little persis-

tence with a hand eyelet plier and 1/4" eyelets will yield a very good result.

The shade is similar to the dowel method, but the open tucks give a very distinctive softened look. It is especially nice in solid colors because the tucks create a design in shadows. Some prints may not be suitable if the tucks break up the design unattractively.

MEASURING

To determine fabric length add 1-1/2" for each horizontal row of rings.

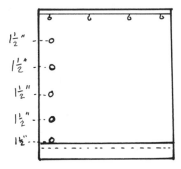

1. Follow steps 1 through 4 for Standard Method, but do not stitch hem.

2. Cut a strip of 3/4" twill tape for each vertical row of eyelets. Cut tapes the length of the shade fabric minus 2".

3. Pin tapes side by side to cutting board or work surface. Draw a line across all tapes 1-3/4" up from the bottom, then every 7-1/2" to mark the tuck location. Then draw a line 3/4" on either side of the tuck marks.

4. Lay shade face down on cutting board or work surface. Slip bottom 1" of tape under hem edge, then pin tapes at center marks on each tuck--making sure the tapes and marks are all even and

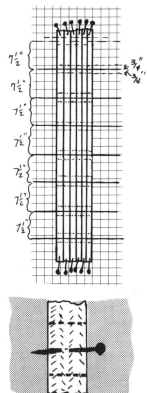

parallel. Stitch top of hem.

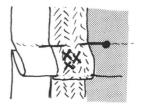

5. Pin each tuck in place using the 3/4" marks as guides. Check from both sides to be sure tuck is pinned even. Remove center pin.

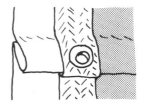

6. Use eyelet plier to punch two or three holes (see x's on illus.) close together to make hole big enough for 1/4" eyelet.

7. Work half of eyelet through the hole in the fabric. Position second half of eyelet and squeeze FIRMLY in place with plier.

8. When eyelets are all in place, a narrow strip of molding (1/8" by 3/8") or an 1/8" dowel may be slipped in behind each tuck and behind side hems. These optional strips help the shade keep its shape and give a little more weight to the tucks.

9. Tie a knot at the end of each stringing cord so it cannot slip thru the eyelet. Then string and mount as for Standard Method steps 8 through 10.

twill tape

6"

eyelets for cords

slat tucked inside side hems

wood slats or dowels optional

Hem Facing

Note: 1/8" eyelets may be used if each tuck is double stitched for reinforcement as shown.

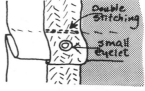

Double Stitching

small eyelet

Hobbled

This shade is like a basic Roman shade except that pleats are folded softly, even when the shade is down. It is a nice method for plain fabrics because the folds add interest and texture, and they hide the stitches that hold the rings in place.

Because of the added amount of fabric, the pleats take up more window space when the shade is pulled. Thus if clearance for a doorway or maximum light is desired, it would be advisable to consider a wall or ceiling mount to allow stacking room for the pleats.

MEASURING

To determine the necessary length, multiply times two.

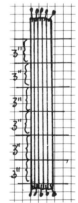

1. Follow directions for Standard Method steps 1 through 5.

2. Cut 1/4" twill tapes for each vertical row of rings. Cut each tape the finished length plus 2".

   Pin tapes to cutting board or work surface. Mark across tapes 1/2" up from bottom, then every 3" (or half the distance between the rings on the shade.)

3. Pin each mark on tape to a corresponding ring mark on the shade, drawing up slack in pleat and forming a fold.

4. Place ring on pin and
zig-zag over ring,
catching just one lay-
er of lining and face
fabric. Do about three
rows at a time, using a
pattern similar to the

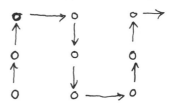

one at right. This seems to work best and wastes the
least thread. Stop and clip off threads, then continue
with next three rows, etc.

5. String and mount
shade same as
for Standard
Method, steps
8 through 10.

NOTE: For a
ringless hobbled
shade, use Gosling
Shade Tape. Tack
to back of shade and
use groups of five cross
threads to form cord sites.
(See pp. 83 and 84.)

Twill tape method

GOSLING TAPE Method

tack twill tape at intervals equal to ½ the distance between rings

thread pulling cord through five cross threads

catch tape and shade in small tuck stitch.

STRINGING VARIATIONS

COUNTERBALANCED SHADE

A student once described to me how she and her husband had
rigged a counterbalanced shade that did not need awning
cleats, but would stay at a given level by lifting or pulling.

The shade is constructed as in the above methods. However
two additional weights are needed, each equal to half the
weight of the rod. (The couple used B-B's in cloth pouches.)

String half the cords in one direction, half in the other. Attach weights to the cords. Now the shade will stay at any point you raise or lower it to, because of the equally counterbalanced weights.

You can conceal the weight pouches with fabric, trim, tassels, etc.

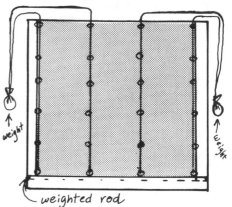

weighted rod

FISHLINE THREADING

Instead of rings and cords, fishline can be sewn through the shade at intervals, run through the screw eyes, and tied off and used to pull the shade.

The line will make a nearly invisible lacing.

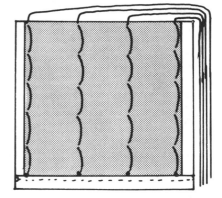

CONTINUOUS CORDING

Reduces cord tension problems which cause shades to hang crooked. Try to use even number of rows of rings. Start with two outside rows of rings. Run cord down one row, across bottom and up other outside row. Next two rows near outside edges are strung using one cord in the same way. Continue till all rows have been strung.

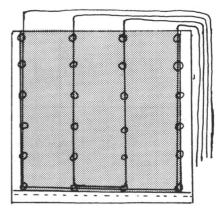

To level a shade raise it and hold it level in one hand while pulling the cords to tighten them with the other.

ACCORDIAN SHADE

This member of the Roman shade family has permanently pleated fabric that resembles a stretched out accordian when the shade is lowered. Cords are run through holes which are punched through the shade fabric.

MEASURING

To determine length cut fabric 1-3/4 times window length. To determine width cut fabric 2" wider than finished width. For backing use iron on roller backing such as Tran Lam (see p. 24) or heavy crisp iron-on non-woven such as Detail Pelomite. Cut backing same as for fabric.

1. Following directions for backing fabric, press shade fabric to backing. (See pp 24 -25 for roller shade backing directions.) Square shade and trim to finished width.

2. Using your cutting board graph or a ruler, lightly mark a line 4-1/4" up from bottom edge, then a line 2" above that, then lines every 4" up the shade.

WRONG SIDE

$4\frac{1}{4}$"

3. Press the 4-1/4" section forward with wrong sides together,
then fold back along the 2" line
and crease sharply.

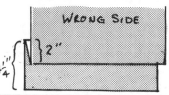

Note: If you are using Tran Lam backing warm the backing
with the iron in the area of the pleat (be sure to use a press
cloth), then quickly fold the pleat into position. The Tran
Lam is soft while warm, and stiffens as it cools.

4. When you come to the end of the shade, leave a 5" extension that folds <u>away</u> from you. The last pleat will be
3" deep and the remaining 2" if for mounting ease.

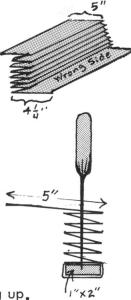

5. Cut 2 1"x2" boards the finished width
of the shade. (Remember a finished
1"x2" piece of lumber is really 1-1/2"
wide.) Wrap the 4-1/4" end around
one of the boards and tack it in place
temporarily.

Take an ice pick or a sharp awl and
drive it through the shade into the
board 6" from the ends (2" on very
narrow shades), and in the center of
the shade. Remove the shade from
the board. You may need to enlarge
the holes if your stringing cords are
large enough to rub on the edges.
Cords must slide freely without hanging up.

6. Drill holes through the board large enough for cord to
pass through. Re-tack the shade to the board. Punch
holes to correspond with holes drilled through board.

7. To make shade conform to window length and to keep
pleats sharp--collapse the shade to window length, cut
a length of 1/2" twill tape or gross grain ribbon the finished length plus 1/4" for each pleat and 2" for ease.

Determine the distance between pleats and staple the
tape just to the edge of the fold directly behind the
line of holes for the cords. Anchor ends of tapes securely to the mounting boards as they help carry the
weight of the shade.

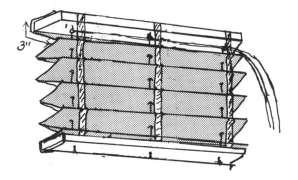

8. Position screw eyes or pulleys on mounting board above
the pulling cords. Staple shade to mounting board.
Cut pulling cords and tie a knot in the end of each one.
String cords by running them through the holes and then
through screw eyes. Mount as for Standard Method
Roman shade.

Note: It is not necessary to use the stapled tapes on the
back of the pleats. However, if you don't, the pleats
will stretch out much flatter as the shade is lowered, los-
ing much of the crisp accordian look. It is a matter of
opinion which method looks best.

CLOUD SHADE

This very soft shade is at its best in soft, lightweight, sheer fabrics. It can be dramatic in lace. While the softness comes through best in unlined versions, lining can be used to give body and protection from sun as well as a uniform look to the outside.

There is somewhat the feeling of a balloon shade, and the softness of an Austrian shade, but it is simpler to make than either one of them.

MEASURING

To determine length use
1. Finished length plus 15" to 24"(for long windows) for shade with poufed bottom when down, or
2. Finished length plus 6-1/2" for straight 'shirred' shade when down.

To determine width multiply finished width times two.

1. Match fabric design and seam if necessary to achieve desired width. Use French seams on sheers.

2. Turn under 1/4" on side edges. Then turn, press and stitch 1" side hems. Turn under 1/4" on bottom edge, then turn, press and stitch a 2-1/2" bottom hem.

3. Turn down top edge 3-3/4". Lay 4-cord shirring tape in place 1/4" down from top folded edge. Stitch just above and below each cord (8 lines of stitching.)

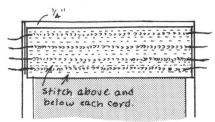

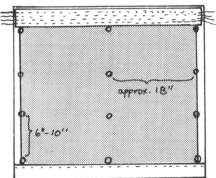

4. Stitch rings in place. Place rings 3/4" in from side edges, one at the top of the hem and one just below the shirring tape. Stitch the remaining rings equally at spaces of 6" to 10". (The larger the space, the bigger the pouf on the shade when pulled.)

Note: The horizontal rows will seem very wide, but will be half that distance when the shirring tape is gathered.

5. Tie knots in the ends of the shirring cords so they can't pull out, then pull cords--drawing up shade to finished width. (On an outside mount, plan for shade to go around the ends of the board.)

6. Prepare a piece of lining fabric 4"x finished width of shade. Fold in half lengthwise to form a 2" strip. Zig-zag or finish edges, then stitch the strip to the 1/4" allowance at the top of the shade above the shirring tape. This will form a flap that can be attached to the mounting board.

7. Cover a 3/8" metal rod with matching fabric. (Fabric may be sewn or glued to the rod.) Then--

   A. Slip the rod through the hem, if a shirred, gathered or poufed look is desired when shade is down.

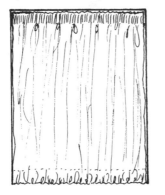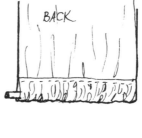

B. Run the rod through the first row of rings
   if a loose curtain look is desired when
   shade is down. Tack rod in place to shade.

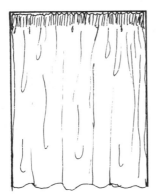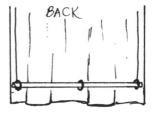

8. String and mount as for Standard Method steps 8 thru 10.

VARIATIONS

Gathered Heading

The use of a casing at the heading of a cloud shade is a fast
and easy alternative. It gives a shade the look of a flat
stretched, shirred panel when down, with soft poufs when

pulled. The shade may be installed on wood drapery poles, or a cafe rod mounted at the front of the mounting board. If a curtain rod is used, it must be very sturdy to withstand the strain when the cords are pulled.

Cut and seam as for method above, however sew a casing at top and bottom of shade. Gather shade onto rod at top and onto weight rod at bottom.

FRONT →

← BACK

Pleated Heading

To give the cloud shade a closer family resemblence to a balloon shade, yet maintain the easy construction, try box pleats along the heading. This variation is slightly poufed when lowered.

MEASURING

To determine length add 15" to finished length. Width is double finished width.

Make 1" side hems. Turn top edge down 1/2" and stitch. Make a bottom hem/casing to hold weight bar. Form equally spaced box pleats at the top of the shade before mounting to the board. Run rod through bottom casing as above, or a covered weight rod may be attached at top edge of bottom hem.

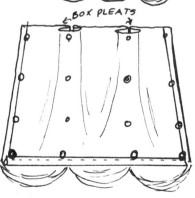

BOX PLEATS

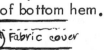

Fabric cover

Note: A casing style cafe curtain can be quickly converted into a cloud shade by adding rings, cords and weight bar. Mount on existing curtain rod. Neat trick for time saving and for apartment dwellers.

Pole Heading with Ruffle

This very attractive variation to the cloud shade is similar to a gathered heading but with a deep stand-up ruffle. The use of a large pole 2" in diameter gives a special effect. The ruffle may be anywhere from 2 to 10 inches in depth. A 6" to 8" ruffle seems to be most effective. The deep ruffle will generally require an outside mount at the window to be most pleasing to the eye. (The ends of the pole should be covered with matching fabric.)

Measuring
To determine length add twice height of ruffle to 1-1/2 x the window height. Width is double finished width.

1. Follow steps I and 2 for basic cloud shade.
2. Turn top edge under 1/4" then turn top casing down to form desired ruffle depth plus casing for pole. Stitch pole casing. Add rings.

6"-8" for heading ruffle

3½" for 2" pole

3. Gather shade onto pole. Top rings must be reinforced to take the strain of the pulling cords. Alternatives include placing screw eyes in the pole or into the window casing directly behind the pole.

4. Cover a 3/8" metal rod with matching fabric. Slip the rod through rings and distribute fabric evenly. Tack rod casing to rings or cover rod with extra fabric at top to attach to rings (See illustration p. 101).

Note: This makes a very elegant treatment when combined with a gathered stand-up ruffled cafe at the bottom of the window. Leave room for cloud to slip behind cafe if lowered.

104

BALLOON SHADE

The balloon shade is related to both Roman and Austrian shades. It is flat in appearance when down, falling from inverted box pleats. It swags and poufs at the bottom when raised.

Balloon shades are enjoying a strong popularity with the softer look in decor, and they have become a symbol of custom decorating. They can be found gracing the pages of many of today's decorating magazines.

Though they may be constructed in almost any fabric, softer types will generally swag more easily and gracefully. Dressing the balloon shade requires pulling the swags out and down as they go up. After awhile they train themselves. Another trick that works well is to hold the bottom rod and swing it out to catch it full of air as you quickly pull up the shade. It really balloons nicely then.

A shorter shade can be constructed to serve as a valance for use with shades, blinds, curtains or drapes. Decorators sometimes tuck tissue paper into balloon valances to help them maintain a full soft look.

MEASURING

To determine length
A) Finished length minus
   5" for a shade that
   hangs flat when down
B) Window opening plus
   10" for a shade that
   will have a pouf at
   the bottom when down.
To determine width the
basic rule is double the
finished width plus 3"
for side hems.
Hem facing strip for both
types is cut 9-1/2" deep
by finished width plus 2",
(Cut two).

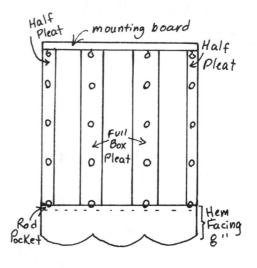

The distance between pleats on a balloon shade is usually
9" to 12". Given a free choice, I would choose 12". For
example on a 36" shade there could be four pleats 9" apart,
or three pleats 12" apart. My choice of 12" means less fabric width, fewer rings and cords, and less time expended.
However, if a seam would fall behind a pleat if I used 9"
but would not be easy to conceal if I used 12", I would consider the change.

It is therefore a good idea to use a piece of fabric or paper
to pre-determine pleat placement. Include seams if they
are necessary and pin and fold the strip to your cutting board
or work surface. (Seams are best hidden somewhere inside
a pleat. Illustrated: 36" shade with three equal pleats.

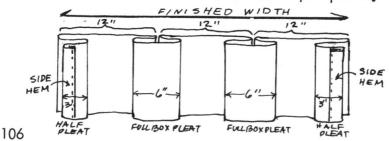

1. Prepare fabric, seaming for added width if needed. Press seams open.

2. Turn under 1/2" on each side edge, then 1" to form 1" side hems. Stitch or fuse hems.

3. Working on cutting board or work surface, with wrong side down, fold box-pleats as follows--one half pleat at each side hem, one full box-pleat at each marked interval in the body of the shade. (See illustration above for example.) Press pleats and pin.

Note: If your fabric resists sharp creases, you may wish to stitch down the edges of the pleats on the underside.

4. Baste 1/2" from top and bottom of shade to hold pleats in line.

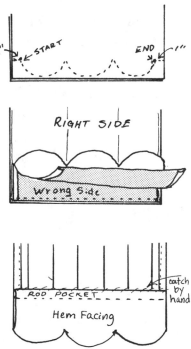

5. Prepare hem facing by placing right sides together and stitching 1/2" seam across bottom. (Hem edge may be shaped or straight.) Fold 1" side extensions in. Press.

6. Place front facing and shade fabric right sides together. Pin and stitch a 1" seam.

7. Turn facing down into position. Press. Fold and press a 1" hem at back top edge. Whip the folded edge into place along the stitching line just made. Then stitch 1" below the top edge of the facing to form a rod pocket. Add trim to bottom edge if desired.

8. String and mount following steps 8 through 10 for Standard Method.

VARIATIONS

Tailored Pleats

In this method a self hem is used, and pleats run clear to the hem. To determine length add 6" to finished length.

Turn up and stitch or fuse a 2" double hem.

Stitch a strip of 1" twill tape a-cross the back of the shade 6" up from bottom edge. This will form the rod pocket.

When using a plain fabric, it is very nice to add some trimming at the top and bottom-- with braid for instance. The object is to give the shade an attractive look when down.

Note: See Pleated Heading on p. 101 for a cloud shade varia-tion that creates a fast, easy, balloon shade look.

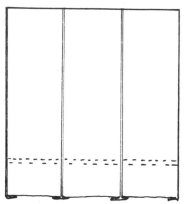

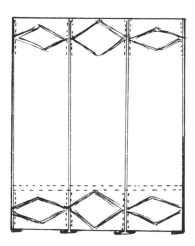

Shirred Top

A strip of fabric shirred with 2 or 4-cord shirring tape can be applied across the top of the shade to soften the look for a special decorative touch.

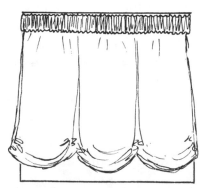

AUSTRIAN SHADES

Softly draped and gathered, Austrian shades make a formal and elegant statement at a window.

If you are interested in a plain, sheer shade my advise generally would be--buy it. But if you want something special and out of the ordinary it will be worth the time and effort to make.

Not long ago I decided to make an Austrian shade from a black and white print polyester interlock knit. I was delighted with the results for a number of reasons. The fabric draped and gathered beautifully, the shade cords did not have to be released for washing, and the shade required no ironing--only a cool dryer and it was ready to hang again.

Obviously the care of the shade is another consideration--cleaning and pressing an Austrian shade is an expensive proposition. A truly easy care shade is worth some initial effort.

MEASURING

To determine amount of fabric needed, first measure window width. Decide how many scallops you want and how wide they need to be to cover the window. (Scallops should not be over 12" wide.)

A. Width

Measure width of window _____

Multiply no. of scallops
times 3" or 4" _____

Plus 3" for side seams
TOTAL WIDTH _____ in.

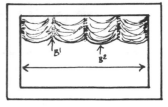

Note: Be sure to allow 1" extra for each seam if fabric must
be seamed to achieve necessary width.

B. LENGTH

For sheers: Window length x 3 = _____ in.
For opaques: Window length x 2 = _____ in.

Note: For mounting decide if finished length is at B-1
top of scallop, or B-2 bottom of scallop. Scallop hangs
down about 3" longer than at B-1.

Ring Tape Method

1. Sew fabric panels together. Use French seams on sheer
   fabrics. Press 1-1/2" hems on sides and bottom. Stitch
   the bottom hem.

2. Cut lengths of ring tape, one more than the number of
   scallops. Knot the ends of the cords so they cannot
   pull out. Pin tapes to shade (glue may be used, but is
   not recommended for sheers.) Be sure rings are even
   and parallel.

3. Start 1-1/2" down
   from top and sew
   on tapes over side
   hems and on body
   of shade. Turn up
   the extra 1" at bot-
   tom and sew into
   loops for weight bar.
   (Your lines of stit-
   ching need not be
   perfect, since they
   will all disappear
   into the gathers.)

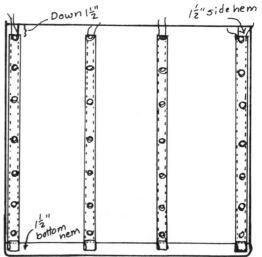

110

4. Since you have allowed up to 4" extra for each scallop, the shade will be much wider at the top than the window. Pin tucks at top on each side of the tapes as shown, until you have eliminated the extra width at top.

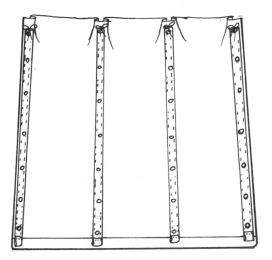

5. A 3/8" metal rod will supply the weight for the shade. The weight is needed to help the shade operate smoothly. To help hold it securely in the loops at the bottom of the shade, first wrap the rod in fabric. You can glue it on, or cut a strip of fabric 2-1/2" wide and 1" longer than the rod. Stitch across the end and along the long edge with 3/8" seam. Turn casing inside out, insert rod and close with hand stitches. Tack rod to loops.

6. Pull the two knotted cords in each tape to gather the shade to the exact length of the window. Knot the cords to prevent gathers from slipping. DO NOT CUT THE CORDS.

When cleaning time comes, you can untie them and flatten the shade for easy

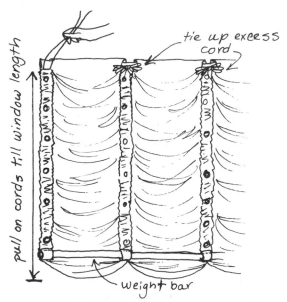

tie up excess cord

pull on cords till window length

weight bar

handling. Make sure all rings are still even across the shade after gathering.

To help even out the gathers and give them a more uniform look, it helps to grasp them on each side of the ring tape and give a firm tug.

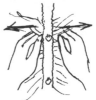

7. To mount and string the shade follow directions for Standard Method Roman shade.

Self Tape Method

This is a particularly arrractive method since tapes are the same color and texture as face fabric, and no tapes will be evident on the back side. Thus it creates a uniform look on the outside of the house. However, it should be noted that it takes a good deal more time to construct this shade than the ring tape method.

Follow directions for ring-tape method with the following exceptions....

1. Make your own 'tapes' by cutting strips of self fabric the length of shade and 2" wide. Fold edges to center & press.

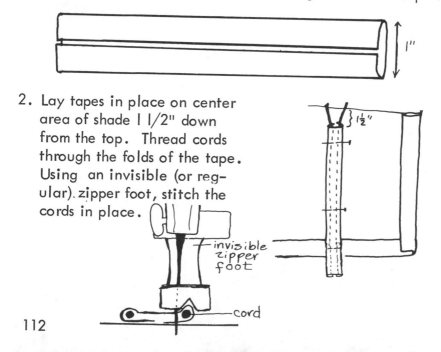

2. Lay tapes in place on center area of shade 1 1/2" down from the top. Thread cords through the folds of the tape. Using an invisible (or regular) zipper foot, stitch the cords in place.

invisible
zipper
foot

cord

3. For hem edges fold and press
   1 1/2" side hem and adjust
   cords as follows:

   1. Stitch 1/2" from edge
      of shade.

   2. Insert two cords within
      the hem. Stitch the
      first cord next to the
      first line of stitching.

   3. Stitch the second cord
      next to the fold.

      The extra fabric on
      center strips will be

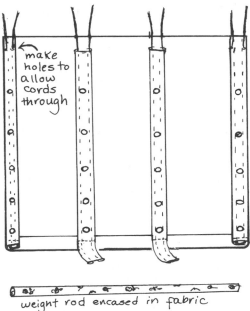

sewn into loops to hold the weight bar. Small separate
strips will have to be sewn to the outside to hold the bar
at those points.

4. Make small holes
   in the side hems to
   allow the cords
   through.

5. Sew rings to the
   tapes at inter-
   vals about 6" a-
   part.

6. When all cords
   and rings are in
   position, pull
   gently, but firmly
   drawing up the
   fabric to the de-
   sired finished
   length. DO NOT CUT THE CORDS. Tie them off securely in neat bundles.

7. Add weight bar and tack it to the loops.

8. Mount and string as for Standard Method Roman shade.

Ringless Tape Method

This method uses Gosling Shade & Ruffling Tape. (See pp. 13, 83 and 84).

1. Follow ring tape method for measuring and preparing fabric. Press 1" side hems. Press and stitch double 1-1/2" bottom hem. Cut tapes same as cut length of shade minus 1-1/2".

2. Lay tapes side by side. Use a felt pen (light color), colored pencil or washable marker. Mark tapes 3" from bottom, then every 12". These guidelines help line gathers up evenly.

3. Pin tapes on shade with side tapes covering hem edges, and 3" mark at top of hem. Stitch each side of tape, backstitching at top of hem, leaving 3" extension.

4. Fold extension into loops to hold weight bar. Stitch securely with small stitches through hem stitches.

5. Zig zag or bias bind top edge of shade.

6. Lift out ends of ruffling threads. Pull threads as you push in gathers with other hand. Work in small sections from tape to tape, until shade is desired length and guide marks are even. Securely knot ruffling threads. (Cut off excess above the knot if you don't need to flatten shade for washing.)

7. Thread tapestry needle with Gosling Cord. Pick up groups of five cross threads (cord sites) with needle. Space them 6" or more depending on fabric and look desired. Use a large eye needle to anchor cords securely at top of hem loop. Add dab of glue to knots to secure.

8. Mount and string shade following directions for Standard Roman Shade.

COACH SHADE

The coach shade is a little hard to categorize. It is a flat rolled shade, but it does not use a roller. It is strung like a Roman shade, but it does not pleat. What it is, is a super simple and adaptable shade. It is great alone, yet it combines well in layered looks. It is at its best in heavy canvas like fabrics, but it can be made in fabrics bonded for more body. This will  mean that the backing fabric will show when the shade is rolled up at the window. Raw cut edges are used at the sides. To prevent raveling they may be treated with zig-zag stitching or a bead of glue. (See p. 40)

The shade is strung with pulling cords, usually in contrasting color, that are visible on the front side. Because the shade is mounted behind the 1 x 2 mounting board, rather than in front, the shade can lie flat and snug to the window or casing, even with an outside mount--a definite energy advantage.

Measuring

Finished length plus 10". Finished width plus 1" or 2". If bonded to a lining, use above dimensions for the lining. For valance prepare a strip of fabric and lining 10" to 12" deep and width of board plus 1".

1. Cut, seam*, and press shade fabric keeping it square. Treat edges for raveling. For bonded fabric, follow directions as for construction of roller shade using the backing of your choice.

*Note: To reduce bulk it is preferable not to have to splice fabric. However, if necessary, seam or overlap and fuse.

2. Attach a 1-1/2" dowel to the bottom edge with tacks or staples. Dowel will be on right side of shade. It may be painted or have circles of fabric glued on ends.

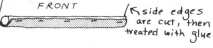

3. Staple shade to top of 1 x 2 mounting board so fabric hangs down the back side of the board.

4. Anchor pulling cords to the back of the board (use a heavy duty staple or U-staples from hardware store.) Outer cords will be fastened about 2" from edges of shade. Another cord at the center of some shades may be desirable. Mount screw eyes on bottom of board in front of cord locations. Cords should be twice length and one must be the width of shade also.

5. Lay valance and lining fabric right sides together. Stitch a 1/2" seam around three sides. Trim, turn and press. Staple to top of board so it falls forward and conceals the screw eyes.

6. Mount shade in window. Secure cords with awning cleat.

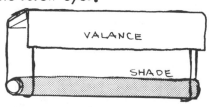

CARE AND UPKEEP

In general shades that are used often won't collect dust and grime. So the best care for all shades is simple-- use them.

Many decorator fabrics have a stain and soil resistor applied during manufacturing. If yours has not, a spray like Skotch-guard, ZePel, or Amway Dri-Guard will keep it fresh longer.

ROLLER SHADES

- Dust them with a soft brush or use a vaccuum cleaner.
- For spot cleaning remove shade from brackets and sponge lightly with damp cloth or treat with spot lifter.
- For more complete cleaning unroll shade ona flat surface. wash it piecemeal using suds (like upholstery shampoo) and while taking care not to abraid the surface. If needed, re-verse shade (being careful not to stretch it while damp) and gently clean the back. Replace in brackets; pull down full length overnight or till thoroughly dry. Roll to top and leave rolled for twelve hours for finished well-groomed look.
- For shades that are not washable, use a wallpaper refresher.
- An art gum eraser can give many shades a quick cleaning.

ROMAN & OTHER TYPES

- Light vacuuming or air fluffing in the dryer keeps them fresh.
- Dry cleaning is recommended over washing to prevent shrink-ing, stretching, distorting. Remove cords to prevent tangling.
- Cleaning in place is highly recommended.
- If you plan to wash your shades, preshrink everything before construction.
- Shades often need 'dressing' to train them into the desired folding and swagging pattern. This may mean smoothing the fabric each time the shade is raised for a while. Soon shades will develop a memory. A product called Spring Mist from drapery or shade shops will also help train fabrics.

HARDWARE/PRODUCT INFO

ANGLE IRON - L-shaped metal support used for mounting all shade types except roller. Available in hardware stores.

AWNING CLEAT - Small metal device attached to side of window frame to secure cords for Roman type shades. Available from drapery and shade shops and marine supply. Also try hardware or home improvement.

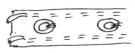

AUSTRIAN SHADE TAPE - Twill tape with woven shirring cords and pre-spaced plastic rings. Used for Austrian shades. Available from fabric and drapery stores.

CARDBOARD CUTTING BOARD - Folding ruled board used for measuring and squaring fabric for all types of shades. Saves time and aids accuracy. Available from fabric departments.

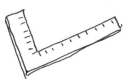

CARPENTER'S SQUARE - Metal L-shaped ruler, used to determine if edges are 'true' and for perfect 90° angles. Useful for all types of shades. Available in hardware departments.

CRAFT/FABRIC GLUE - Tacky, fast-drying, remain flexible when dry. These make excellent timesavers for working with fabric. Wilhold, Quik, Fab Trim, Mighty Tacky.

CORSAGE PINS - Slender 1-1/2" glass headed pins from floral supply make the greatest decorator sewing pins.

DOWELS - Wood dowels of various dia-
meters give shape and dimension to several
Roman shade variations. They are often
warped, so select them carefully. From
lumber store, home improvement centers.

EYELETS - 1/8" and 1/4" eyelets from
notions are used on several Roman shade
variations.

EYELET PLIER - Plier punches hole and sets
eyelets. Select type that uses both 1/8"
and 1/4" eyelets. Available in notions.

FUSIBLE WEB - Meltable webs of synthetic
fibers. Placed between objects, heated
with iron, they melt and fuse materials together. From fabric departments - Stitch
Witchery, Sav-A-Stitch, Poly Web, etc.

LAMINATING GLUE - For gluing fabric to
roller shades or other surfaces. Available
in quarts and gallons from shade shops.
Makes excellent craft glue.

MOUNTING BOARD - Usually a piece of
finished 1"x2" (dimensions are actually
smaller) from lumber yard. For mounting
all shade types except roller.

PLASTIC OR CABONE RINGS - 1/2" and
5/8" rings are best for Roman shades. Found
packaged in notions and knitting supplies.
Some suppliers sell them individually.

ROLLERS - Available from shade shops and
some mail order catalogs. For roller shades.

ROMAN SHADE RING TAPE - Twill tape with pre-spaced plastic rings. Sew tape to fabric, run cord up thru rings causing shade to pleat as it is drawn. From fabric stores.

SCREW EYES - Available from hardware stores in wide range of sizes and strengths, used for stringing Roman type shades.

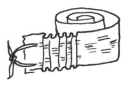

SHIRRING TAPE - Woven tape with heavier cords woven into the construction. Sew flat to fabric, pull up cords and fabric gathers automatically. Used for decorative heading on many shades. From fabric and drapery.

STAPLE GUN AND STAPLES - Handy hardware department item for applying fabric to all types of objects and for mounting Roman and other shades.

TENSION ROD - Curtain rod with rubber tipped feet and spring action that allows it to be placed between surfaces with no holes needed for hanging. From drapery dept.

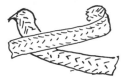

TWILL TAPE - Pre-packaged polyester in 1/4" and 3/4" will be most used for Roman shades and Hobbled shades primarily. Located in notions departments.

WEIGHT ROD - 3/8" solid metal bar used for weight at bottom of Roman type shades. Purchase from drapery or shade shop, or try iron works and home improvement dept.

METRIC EQUIVALENCY CHART

This chart gives the standard equivalents as approved by the Pattern Fashion Industry.

Converting Inches into Millimeters and Centimeters. (Slightly rounded for your convenience.)

mm = millimeters   cm = centimeters   m = meters

inches	mm/cm		inches	cm
⅛	3mm		18	46
¼	6mm		19	48,5
⅜	1cm		20	51
½	1,3cm		21	53,5
⅝	1,5cm		22	56
¾	2cm		23	85,5
⅞	2,2cm		24	61
1	2,5cm		25	63,5
1¼	3,2cm		26	66
1½	3,8cm		27	68,5
1¾	4,5cm		28	71
2	5cm		29	73,5
2½	6,5cm		30	76
3	7,5cm		31	79
3½	9cm		32	81,5
4	10cm		33	84
4½	11,5cm		34	86,5
5	12,5cm		35	89
5½	14cm		36	91,5
6	15cm		37	94
7	18		38	96,5
8	20,5		39	99
9	23		40	101,5
10	25,5		41	104
11	28		42	106,5
12	30,5		43	109
13	33		44	112
14	35,5		45	114,5
15	38		46	117
16	40,5		47	119,5
17	43		48	122
			49	124,5
			50	127

OTHER TITLES BY THE AUTHOR

ENERGY SAVING DECORATING

by Judy Lindahl. 128 pages of simple do-it-yourself instructions and ideas for creating a more energy efficient home. From psychological decorating to retro-fitting a Roman shade to improve its energy efficiency--Don't miss this exciting and timely new book.
© 1981 $6.95

DECORATING WITH FABRIC/An Idea Book

by Judy Lindahl. 128 pages of helpful hints and practical suggestions for how to put fabric on practically anything. Includes: starched walls, quick drapes, pillows galore, folding screens, stretcher bar art, bath accessories, and much more.
A timeless resource to use again and again.
Revised   © 1980 $6.95

To order Decorating With Fabric/An Idea Book, The Shade Book, or Energy Saving Decorating write for information to Judy Lindahl, 3211 NE Siskiyou, Portland, OR 97212 USA or enclose $6.95 per title plus $1.00 postage and handling. Canadian orders must be in U.S. Funds.